EVOLUTIONARY ETHICS

Evolutionary Ethics

A. G. N. FLEW
Professor of Philosophy, University of Keele

MACMILLAN

ST MARTIN'S PRESS

© A. G. N. Flew 1967

First edition 1967
Reprinted (with corrections) 1970

Published by
MACMILLAN AND CO LTD
London and Basingstoke
Associated companies in New York Toronto
Dublin Melbourne Johannesburg and Madras

Library of Congress catalog card no. 68–10637

SBN (paper) 333 03988 2

Printed in Great Britain by
RICHARD CLAY (THE CHAUCER PRESS), LTD
Bungay, Suffolk

CONTENTS

EDITOR'S PREFACE

Few, if any, now share the confidence of some nineteenth-century thinkers that, by a process as inevitable as the survival of the fittest in the animal kingdom, those principles of action and traits of character which are morally best will progressively triumph over all other elements in human nature until man becomes perfect. Nevertheless, there has recently been a considerable revival of interest in the bearing of evolution upon ethics. The study of evolution undoubtedly tells us a great deal about the nature and potentialities of man. Does it also clarify for us the nature of the good at which men should aim? Does it enable us to understand more precisely the meaning of moral judgments concerning what ought, or ought not, to be done? Some modern thinkers have answered yes to such questions; others equally emphatically, no.

Professor Flew has written a critical study of evolutionary ethics which is remarkable both for the scholarship with which he reviews this field and the precision with which he brings the important issues into focus. He covers ground from Darwin to Waddington; and he contributes forcefully to the re-examination of what is often called 'the *is–ought* problem', taking full account of recent work on this subject. His monograph provides students of moral philosophy with a valuable introduction to this important branch of ethics; but it will be of interest to a much wider circle of readers and especially to those who wish to know how far biological science can assist man in his quest for the good life.

University of Exeter   W. D. HUDSON

With the one exception of Newton's *Principia* no single book of empirical science has ever been of more importance to philosophy than this work of Darwin.

JOSIAH ROYCE,
The Spirit of Modern Philosophy (p. 286)

The Darwinian theory has no more to do with philosophy than has any other hypothesis of natural science.

LUDWIG WITTGENSTEIN,
Tractatus Logico-Philosophicus (4.1122)

I. INTRODUCTION

The obvious and the right place from which to begin a study of evolutionary ethics is the work of Charles Darwin. For, primarily, it is his ideas — or what have been thought to be his ideas — which advocates of evolutionary ethics or evolutionary politics have tried to apply more widely. This is not, of course, to say that Darwin had no intellectual ancestors; any more than it is to suggest that biological theory has since his death stood still. To say or to suggest either thing would be absurdly wrong.

It would not even be true to say that nothing was published with any claim to the label 'evolutionary ethics' until after the appearance in 1859 of *The Origin of Species*. For Herbert Spencer was strictly correct when, in the General Preface to *The Principles of Ethics*, he claimed, 'as a matter of historical truth, that in this case, as in other cases, the genesis of ideas does not follow the order of logical sequence; and that the doctrine of organic evolution in its application to human character and intelligence, and, by implication, to society, is of earlier date than *The Origin of Species*'.[1] He is referring here to his *Social Statics*, first issued at the end of 1850 and containing the outline of the ethical ideas which he is about to develop. He could also, and elsewhere does, claim to have been the first to use the notion of the survival of the fittest in an evolutionary context — in the *Westminster Review* for 1852. Again, as has been pointed out long since,[2] the very phrase 'a struggle for existence', which epitomises the gladiatorial view of human life so often taken to be the true moral of Darwinism, is to be found already in a similar context in 1798 in Malthus's *First Essay*,[3] a work to which — as Darwin acknowledged, though he would never have used so portentous a phrase, especially of himself — 'I owe in large measure the stimulation of my thoughts.'[4]

Nevertheless, after all due cautions have been given, it is *The Origin of Species* which is, and must be, the reference point. It is the ideas of this book which the forerunners foreran. It is what this book said or suggested that later evolutionary thinkers tried to develop. It was the triumph in biology of the theory which it presented that lent vicarious prestige to whatever could be put forward as Darwinian.

This explains why the second of the four Sections into which the present monograph is divided will deal with Darwin's theory. The reason why these preliminaries will be fairly extended is that it is essential to master Darwin's general ideas in biology before attempting to consider their application, or misapplication, elsewhere; just as it should be a precondition of either a search for his precursors, or an investigation of the character and extent of later developments, first to get quite straight about what those precursors are supposed to be precursors of, and what the developments are developments from. Although these are all points too obvious to be denied, they are certainly not always acted upon.

After these preliminaries the main treatment in the later sections will be systematic rather than historical. There has been no spokesman for an evolutionary ethic of sufficient stature as a moral thinker to warrant the full individual treatment required by an Aristotle, a Hume, or a Kant. Nor does there seem to have been in such ethics any line of development which it would be philosophically profitable to pursue. Nevertheless — in defiance of all the strict academic compartmentalists, insisting that nothing must have anything to do with anything else — attempts to bring ethics and politics into some sort of relation with the facts of evolutionary biology are perennial; and there has certainly been far too little careful and sympathetic philosophical investigation of what the possibilities and impossibilities here actually are. We shall be having many sharp things to say about some particular sorts of attempt at an evolutionary ethics. So it is the more important to emphasise right from the beginning that the desires to connect, and to see microcosms in relation to the macrocosm, are in themselves excellent; and quite certainly should be shared, and not despised, by anyone who aspires to the title of 'philosopher'. It is, therefore, neither surprising nor discreditable that in every generation since Darwin some of the liveliest and least blinkered of students of biology — Darwin himself included — should have wanted to explore the possibility of connections between evolution and ethics.

The main reason why professional philosophers are apt very brusquely to dismiss all such efforts is that they mistake that they must involve what they call the Naturalistic Fallacy. The nerve of this is an attempt to deduce a conclusion about what *ought* to be, or *ought* to have been, from premises stating only what in neutral fact *is* the case, or what *has been* or what *will be*. Once this fallacy has been recognised for what it is, it may seem that with evolutionary ethics this is both the heart of the matter and the end of the affair: 'There is a temptation for the logician to point out the fallacy and to leave it at that.'[5]

This is not good enough. Nor to finish the job is it sufficient, as the author of that last quotation seems to have thought, straightway to seek for psychogenetic explanations of the supposed mistake in logic. The first thing is to show in some detail precisely what if anything is going wrong in the particular case, or perhaps in several specimen cases, and to identify and to expose any other associated errors and confusions which may have made it easier to effect the illegitimate transition. The second and the more important thing, before the philosopher thinks of launching out into psychogenetic speculations, is to enquire whether there may not after all be something else involved besides this old familiar Naturalistic Fallacy.

Once this question is put, and pressed, it soon becomes obvious that other things are involved. Our Section III therefore raises the questions of whether Darwin's theory could provide a foundation for, or whether it itself contains, a law of progress; in each case arguing for the negative answer. This provides a first occasion to analyse precisely what is and what is not involved in the idea of natural selection, and to distinguish different sorts of law (senses of 'law'). The same section examines extensively two bold attempts. The first is that of Julian Huxley, who began by trying to detect in the actual course of biological evolution trends we could scarcely refuse to count as progressive, and then conscripted these to serve as a reassuring prop such as could in fact be provided only by a natural force or by Divine Providence. The second is that of the Marxist biologist Joseph Needham, who began by discerning in that same actual development the appropriate fulfilment of a universal law of progress, and then tried, despite the supposed inevitability of the socialist apocalypse, to make some room for a measure of historically relevant human choice.

It will perhaps be remarked that both these spokesmen of different sorts of evolutionary ethics, and indeed most of the others considered elsewhere in this monograph, are not merely English-speaking but English. This limitation is an expression of a considered policy. We have deliberately chosen to treat a few fairly fully — and those few the ones most likely to have been read by English-speaking, and particularly British, students — rather than to give a breathless series of mentions of many more. It is in any case hopeless to think of forestalling the complaints of reviewers about the comparative or total neglect of some favoured contributor to what has long since become an unmanageably abundant international literature. What can reasonably be aspired after is that this restrictive policy will make for a more adequate treatment and illustration of the main general issues; and certainly, in a less conciliatory vein, the present writer cannot regret the consequence of having to ignore Teilhard de Chardin in favour of such forthright and immensely more readable authors as Needham and the early Julian Huxley.

Section III, as we have seen, will thus consider the quest in biological evolution for some immanent substitute for Divine Providence. It is only after this that we shall proceed in Section IV to look in a concentrated way at the hardy perennial attempts to proceed directly from the purely factual premises supplied by the science of biology to evaluative conclusions. One key distinction here, often neglected, is that between trying to deduce such conclusions directly from such premises — a move which must involve the Naturalistic Fallacy — and attempting after first somehow establishing a biological criterion to reach them indirectly — an enterprise which might perhaps succeed in escaping this stock objection.

In Section IV too we notice the remarkable variety of moral and

4

political conclusions which their protagonists have believed to be warranted by Darwin's theory. The very diversity, and often mutual incompatibility, of such supposed implications must constitute a strong reason for challenging the legitimacy of the sort of derivation proposed — a type of direct deduction which should already and independently have been seen to be invalid.

Two examples here will sufficiently illustrate this diversity. First, Darwin has been taken, or mistaken, to have provided a knock-down justification for just that same intensely competitive economic system whence, according to Engels and others, he had himself abstracted those ideas of natural selection and of a struggle for existence which he proceeded to employ so triumphantly in his own scientific field.[6] Thus J. D. Rockefeller, who was certainly an expert both on big business and on no-holds-barred competition, in one of his Sunday-school addresses declared: 'The growth of a large business is merely a survival of the fittest. . . . The American Beauty rose can be produced in the splendour and fragrance which bring cheer to its beholder only by sacrificing the early buds which grow up around it. This is not an evil tendency in business. It is merely the working out of a law of nature and a law of God.'[7]

Second, Darwin has also been taken, or mistaken, to have provided the premises to sustain the opposite conclusions of collectivism. Such a moral seems to have been suggested, albeit cryptically, by the other founding father of Marxism when he read the *Origin* at its first publication.[8] By the turn of the century it had become a commonplace of socialist propaganda. Thus in 1905, in an Editor's Preface to a work on *Socialism and Positive Science* first published in Rome in 1894 and already widely circulated on the Continent, James Ramsay MacDonald stated that 'the Conservative and aristocratic interests in Europe have armed themselves for defensive and offensive purposes with the law of the struggle for existence, and its corollary, the survival of the fittest. Ferri's aim in this volume has been to show that Darwinism is not only not in intellectual opposition to Socialism, but is its scientific foundation.'[9] MacDonald goes on to conclude that 'Socialism is naught but Darwinism economised, made definite, become an

intellectual policy, applied to the conditions of human society'.[10]
It is noteworthy, both as one of those paradoxical reversals which
are so common in the history of ideas, and as a further indication
of the unwisdom of trying directly to deduce norms from facts,
that Ferri himself begins by proclaiming himself 'a convinced
follower' not only of Marx but also of both 'Darwin and Spencer'.
He allows 'that Darwin, and especially Spencer, stopped short
half-way from the final conclusions of religious, political and social
order, which necessarily follow from their indisputable premises'.[11]
But, notwithstanding his recognition that 'Herbert Spencer
affirmed aloud his English individualism', Ferri still insists on
concluding that 'Marx completes the work of Darwin and
Spencer'.[12]

Finally, Section V is about 'Seeing in an Evolutionary Perspective'. Sections III and IV discuss fairly strong views of the 'philosophical implications' of Darwin's theory. Section V is concerned
with the weaker, more defensible, and unduly neglected conten-
tions, that the practical thinker needs ever to remember that
ethical ideas have evolved and will presumably continue to evolve,
and that all human life — and questions of public and private
conduct in particular — can fruitfully be seen in an evolutionary
perspective. It is, we shall argue, in the development of such relatively mild and vegetarian notions — rather than in those of a
reinforcement by a surrogate Providence or of the deduction of
morality from biology — that we have to seek whatever residue of
merit there may be in the bolder programmes of evolutionary
ethics.

II. DARWIN'S THEORY

Darwin is so often thought of as the sponsor of 'the Theory of Evolution' that it is salutary to recall the full title of *The Origin*. It is *The Origin of Species by Means of Natural Selection*; and to this is added a sub-title, which has since acquired a sinister ring: *or the Preservation of Favoured Races in the Struggle for Life*. Darwin's claim to originality does not lie in his having been the first to entertain the possibility of the evolution, as opposed to the special creation, of species. 'The general hypothesis of the derivation of all present species from a small number, or perhaps a single pair, of original ancestors was propounded by the President of the Berlin Academy of Sciences, Maupertuis, in 1745 and 1751, and by the principal editor of the *Encyclopédie*, Diderot, in 1749 and 1754.'[13] Nor was Darwin the first to introduce into a biological context the ideas of natural selection and of a struggle for existence. These can be found in Lucretius in the first century B.C., although he combines them with a notion of natural kinds detached from that of special creation — or indeed any creation by any genuinely personal agency. Lucretius describes how in the infancy of the earth it 'put forth herbage and trees first, and in the next place created the generations of mortal creatures, arising in many kinds. . . . Wherefore again and again the earth deserves the name of mother which she has gotten, since of herself she created the human race, and produced almost at a fixed time every animal that ranges wild over the great mountains, and the birds of the air at the same time in all their varied forms. . . . Many were the monsters also that the earth then tried to make, springing up with wondrous appearance and frame: the hermaphrodite, between man and woman yet neither, different from both; some without feet, others again bereft of hands; some found dumb also without a mouth, some blind without face. . . . So with the rest of like monsters and portents that she made, it was all in vain: since nature denied them growth, and they could not attain the desired flower of age nor find food nor join by the ways of Venus.' Lucretius concludes: 'And many species of animals must have perished at that time, unable by procreation to forge out the chain of posterity; for whatever you see feeding on the breath of life, either cunning or courage or at least quickness must have kept that kind from its earliest existence.'[14] And of course, Lucretius was himself a disciple, clothing in Latin verse ideas which he had learned from the fourth-century Greek Epicurus, who was here himself using such fifth-century sources as Empedocles of Acragas.[15]

Yet none of this diminishes either the originality or the importance of Darwin's work. What he did was to bring the key ideas together into an argument, and to illustrate that argument with an enormous mass of evidence, much of it the product of his own observations. As he himself remarked, in a typically modest and engaging passage of the *Autobiography*, '*The Origin of Species* is one long argument from the beginning to the end, and it has convinced not a few able men.'[16]

One recent interpreter goes so far as to say: 'The old arguments for evolution were only based on circumstantial evidence. . . . But the core of Darwin's argument was of a different kind. It did not make it more probable — it made it a certainty. Given his facts his conclusion *must* follow: like a proposition in geometry. You do not show that any two sides of a triangle are very *probably* greater than the third. You show they *must* be so. Darwin's argument was a *de*ductive one — whereas an argument based on circumstantial evidence is *in*ductive.'[17] This statement is certainly correct in so far as it insists that Darwin's argument has a deductive core, although it surely exaggerates the amount which this core by itself establishes.

Consider Darwin's Introduction. He first presents his problem: 'In considering the origin of species, it is quite conceivable that a naturalist, reflecting on the mutual affinities of organic beings, on their embryological relations, their geographical distribution, geological succession, and other such facts, might come to the conclusion that species had not been independently created, but had descended, like varieties, from other species. Nevertheless such a conclusion, even if well-founded, would be unsatisfactory, until it could be shown how the innumerable species inhabiting this world have been modified, so as to acquire that perfection of structure and coadaptation which justly excites our admiration.'[18] Then, after a sharp paragraph, excised from later editions, about 'the author of the *Vestiges of Creation*', Darwin continues: 'It is, therefore, of the highest importance to gain a clear insight into the means of modification and coadaptation. At the commencement of my observations it seemed to me probable that a careful study of domesticated animals and of cultivated plants would offer the best chance of making out this obscure problem. Nor have I been disappointed. . . . I shall devote the first chapter . . . to "Variation under Domestication". We shall thus see that a large amount of hereditary modification is at least possible.'[19]

Chapter ii is to deal with 'Variation under Nature'. 'In the next chapter the "Struggle for Existence" amongst all organic beings throughout the world, which inevitably follows from the high geometrical ratio of their increase, will be considered. . . . As many more individuals of each species are born than can possibly survive; and as, consequently, there is a frequently recurring struggle for existence, it follows that any being if it vary however slightly in any manner profitable to itself, under the complex and sometimes varying conditions of life, will have a better chance of surviving, and thus be *naturally selected*. From the strong principle of inheritance, any selected variety will tend to propagate in its new and modified form. This fundamental subject of "Natural Selection" will be treated at some length in the fourth chapter; and we shall then see how natural selection almost inevitably causes much extinction of the less improved forms of life, and leads to what I have called divergence of character. In the next chapter I shall discuss the complex and little known "Laws of Variation".'[20] The five following chapters consider the most obvious and serious difficulties in the way of accepting the theory, and the final one is a 'Recapitulation and Conclusion'.

This sketch of the argument and plan of the book indicates both what the deductive core of that argument was, and that Darwin himself was not inclined to think that that core constituted a demonstration of his main conclusions. He does not claim to have demonstrated, and did not in fact demonstrate, 'the conclusion that species had not been independently created, but had descended, like varieties, from other species'. Nor did he claim to have demonstrated 'how the innumerable species inhabiting this world have been modified, so as to acquire that perfection of structure and coadaptation which justly excites our admiration'. But what he did succeed in demonstrating was that, granted as premises certain very general and scarcely disputable facts, then some natural selection must also be a fact.

Thus in chapter iii Darwin argues: 'A struggle for existence inevitably follows from the high rate at which all organic beings tend to increase . . . as more individuals are produced than can possibly survive, there must in every case be a struggle for existence, either one individual with another of the same species, or with the individuals of a different species, or with the physical conditions of life. It is the doctrine of Malthus applied with manifold force to the whole animal and vegetable kingdoms, for in this case there can be no artificial increase of food, and no prudential restraint from marriage.'[21] Just as the idea of the struggle for existence is derived as a consequence of the combination of a geometrical ratio of increase with the finite possibilities of survival, so in chapter iv 'Natural Selection' is itself derived as a consequence of the combination of the struggle for existence with variation. Darwin summarises his argument: 'If . . . organic beings present individual differences in almost every part of their structure, and this cannot be disputed; if there be, owing to their geometrical rate of increase, a severe struggle for existence at some age, season, or year, and this certainly cannot be disputed; then . . . it would be a most extraordinary fact if no variations had ever occurred useful to each being's own welfare, in the same manner as variations have occurred useful to man. But if variations useful to any organic being do occur, assuredly individuals thus characterised will have the best chance of being preserved in the struggle for life; and from the strong principle of inheritance they will tend to produce offspring similarly characterised. This principle of preservation, or the survival of the fittest, I have called natural selection.'[22]

Yet to prove this strictly is not strictly to prove that all species are 'descended, like varieties, from other species'. Darwin proceeds in the next paragraph but one to state: 'Whether natural selection has really thus acted in adapting the various forms of life to their several conditions and stations, must be judged by the general tenor and balance of evidence given in the following chapters.' This advice is clearly correct. For the demonstration as given leaves open such theoretical possibilities as that there might turn out to be comparatively narrow limits on the amount of change which could in practice come about in this sort of way, or that a Creator might have chosen to create some or all species specially — perhaps also, and perhaps inevitably, arranging at the same time for false clues which would discomfit the incautious infidel.[23]

Nor, even when these arbitrary suppositions have been suitably disposed of, can it be allowed that Darwin has demonstrated that natural selection operating on chance variations has been solely and entirely responsible for all 'that perfection of structure and coadaptation which justly excites our admiration'. He himself makes no such claim. In the last sentence of the Introduction, after a cautious statement of an evolutionary view and a repudiation of his earlier belief that 'each species has been independently created', he writes: 'I am convinced that natural selection has been the most important, but not the exclusive, means of modification.'[24] Indeed, to the surprise of some of those who know the ferocity with which neo-Darwinians are apt to reject anything which smacks of Lamarck, Darwin himself, though — and perhaps partly because — he insisted that 'Our ignorance of the laws of variation is profound',[25] always allowed the possibility that the effects of use and disuse may be inherited: 'my critics frequently assume that I attribute all changes of corporal structure and mental power exclusively to the natural selection of such variations as are often called spontaneous; whereas, even in the first edition of *The Origin of Species* I distinctly stated that great weight must be attributed to the inherited effects of use and disuse, with respect both to the body and the mind.'[26]

What Darwin did do was to bring various very general facts and key notions together into a deductive argument, showing by this and by appeal to other more direct considerations that natural selection must be and is going on. This granted, he is able to deploy a massive case for saying that species have evolved, and that natural selection has been — and is — the main instrument of this evolution. The variations upon which this selection works are, he always insists, all individually small: 'As natural selection acts solely by accumulating slight, successive, favourable variations, it can produce no great or sudden modifications . . .'; and this squares well with 'the canon of "Natura non facit saltum" [Nature does not make leaps] which every fresh addition to our knowledge tends to confirm'.[27] Darwin is already in the *Origin* cautiously willing to extend his account to all species, except apparently the first: 'I believe that animals are descended from at m os only four or five progenitors, and plants from an equal or lesser number. Analogy would lead me one step farther, namely, to the belief that all animals and plants are descended from some one prototype. But analogy may be a deceitful guide. Nevertheless . . . we must . . . admit that all the organic beings which have ever lived on this earth may be descended from some one primordial form.'[28]

III. A LAW OF PROGRESS?

One great advantage of starting, as we have insisted on doing, from Darwin himself is that this helps to bring out the fundamental difference between evolution and natural selection. Another is that it focuses attention on the deductive core of Darwinism. No one who has failed to appreciate these two things can hope to do precise justice to the nature and the originality of Darwin's contribution. For our present purposes they are equally important, but in other ways. It is the notion of evolution, and the consequent discrediting of the idea of special interventions in the biological sphere, which promises to reinforce our suspicions of those who would claim that supernatural activity endorses (favoured) moral intuitions and the deliverances of (privileged) consciences. It is similarly this same notion of evolution which applied to ethical ideas must discourage any assumption of an authoritative finality, in principle beyond all criticism and reappraisal. It is the fact that the core of Darwin's theory is a compulsive deductive argument which makes it possible to misplace the idea of necessity, and then perhaps to mistake its character: where a conclusion follows necessarily it can be all too easy to assume that that conclusion must itself be logically, or even morally, necessary. When an appreciation of the deductive character of this argument is combined with a failure fully to understand how restricted is the meaning in this context of such phrases as 'the survival of the fittest' and 'natural selection', it may appear as if Darwin has established some sort of law of progress — a misconception from which Darwin himself was not, as we shall soon find, quite emancipated.

(i) THE MEANING OF THE EXPRESSION 'THE SURVIVAL OF THE FITTEST'

This expression — as has been noticed already — was originally coined by Herbert Spencer. But when employed within the context

13

of Darwin's theory its meaning is restricted. For that theory provides no independent criterion of fitness. It is, as has very frequently but too often ineffectively been pointed out, a theory of the survival of the fittest only and precisely in so far as actual or possible survival is to be construed as the sufficient condition of fitness to survive. If some further and independent criterion were to be introduced the deductive argument would no longer be valid: natural selection is necessarily selection only for exactly what at precisely the time in question it in fact takes to survive; and where anything else seems to be being picked it is because that something else then happens to be linked contingently with what at that time happens to be required for survival. The Darwinian guarantee that it is always the fittest who have survived, the fittest who do survive, and the fittest who will survive is by itself neither an assurance that any particular thing which has survived so far will continue to do so, nor an undertaking that everything which is most worth while must survive. If anyone were to complain, using this present Darwinian criterion of fitness, that some particular social arrangement encourages the multiplication of the unfit and the extermination of the fit, then his complaint would be plainly self-contradictory. It seems to be peculiarly difficult to keep this last observation clearly and consistently in mind. Even so shrewd a commentator as Professor D. G. Ritchie, in his *Darwinism and Politics*, at least seems to lapse in the remark that the 'prudential restraint' of Malthus 'would mean that the most careful and intelligent part of the population would leave the continuance of the race mainly to the least careful and least intelligent portion — thus bringing about the survival of the unfittest'.[29] This uncharacteristic lapse, if it really is a lapse, is all the more noteworthy in that the author had earlier been at pains to point out, following T. H. Huxley, that 'the fittest' here means only 'those "best fitted to cope with their circumstances" in order to survive and transmit offspring'; and had even himself gone on to make, against Herbert Spencer, the further point that it must be contradictory 'to blame governments simply because they "interfere" with natural laws'.[30] (Perhaps in this particular case it would be not merely charitable but also correct to construe Ritchie's 'the survival of the unfittest' here as an elliptical equivalent of '(what by any sane standards of human worth would be) the survival of the unfittest'.

The same and further difficulties arise about 'natural selection', which in Darwin is an alternative expression for 'the survival of the fittest': 'This principle of preservation, or the survival of the fittest, I have called natural selection.'[31] For here we have also to recognise not only that the occurrence of natural selection necessarily guarantees, because it is logically equivalent to, the survival of the fittest, but also that the achievement of Darwin's theory is precisely to show that such selection, as a matter of fact, constitutes an immensely effective instrument which — given the necessary variations, and in inordinate time — has produced fabulous results. When we also take into the reckoning the fact that many people are inclined to believe, that whatever is in any sense natural must be as such commendable, and that Nature is a deep repository of wisdom, we need not be surprised to discover that for many the process of evolution by natural selection becomes a secular surrogate for Divine Providence; and that for some the possibility, or even the duty, of relying on this benign and mighty force presents itself as a decisive reason why positive social policies must be superfluous, and may be wrong — indeed almost blasphemous![32]

(ii) THE MEANING OF THE EXPRESSION 'NATURAL SELECTION'

In this the wheel turns full circle. For the greatest philosophical significance of Darwin's work — in a sense of 'philosophy' both much wider and more usual than that affected by the Wittgenstein of the *Tractatus* — lies precisely in the fact that Darwin showed how the appearances of design among living things might come about without actual design.[33] The whole point about natural selection is, one is tempted to say, that it is not selection at all. Indeed someone might well have urged — someone probably has — that natural selection is really an empty idea, because strictly the expression 'natural selection' is self-contradictory. Here one may recall and compare the argument, which was at one time used against Freud, that the notion of an unconscious mind is self-contradictory, because a mind is essentially something which thinks and because, on a similarly Cartesian definition, 'thinking' is a generic term for all and only modes of consciousness. With natural selection the line would be that choice or selection is essentially artificial, as opposed to natural; and it is both as such and for independent reasons necessarily a prerogative of persons.

In either case such arguments, even if strictly correct, are as objections pedantic and perverse. For both Freud and Darwin were drawing attention to enormously fruitful analogies: on the one hand between certain patterns of behaviour which are and others which are not accompanied by consciousness;[34] and on the other hand between the intentional activities of animal- and plant-breeders, and the unplanned and undirected operations of living nature in general. Certainly in the Darwinian case much of the pungent appeal of the label 'natural selection' derives from the very fact that the expression is strictly contradictory. The tension between its two elements gives it the appeal of such a paradoxical idiom as 'the evidence of my own eyes', which makes the point that I, having actually seen it myself, have something much more direct and better than what usually counts as evidence. Yet there should be no doubt, despite some recent suggestions to the contrary,[35] that in its Darwinian employment the expression 'natural selection' does have content; and that the assertion that natural selection occurs is none the less contingent and empirically falsifiable for being beyond all reasonable doubt true.

To state that natural selection occurs is to make at least three claims: first, that not all offspring survive to reproduce; second, although most creatures reproduce after their kind, variations do nevertheless occur; and third, the character of these variations is relevant to questions about which offspring will survive to reproduce. The factual character of the first, and the difference to be made by the conjunction with it of the equally factual second and third, can be illustrated by some famous lines from *In Memoriam* (1850), in which we see the first clearly without a glimmering of the other two:

So careful of the type she seems,
So careless of the single life;

> . . . of fifty seeds,
> She often brings but one to bear,
> I falter where I firmly trod, . . .
> 'So careful of the type'? but no,
> From scarped cliff and quarried stone
> She cries, 'A thousand types are gone:
> I care for nothing, all shall go'.[36]

The danger of Darwin's pointedly paradoxical expression 'natural selection' — and this danger has often been realised — is that it may mislead people to overlook that this sort of selection is blind and non-rational; precisely that is the point. Once this point is missed it is easy, especially if you are already apt to see Nature as a mentor, to go on to take natural selection as a sort of supreme court of normative appeal; and this despite — or in many cases doubtless because of — the time-serving character of the criterion of fitness by which this sort of selection operates. Such ideas may then be, and often have been, regarded as the biological application of the Hegelian slogan 'World history is the world's court of judgment'.[37]

(iii) PROGRESS IN DARWIN'S THEORY?

These apotheoses of natural selection take many forms. Perhaps the most interesting and important of such misconceptions, and one from which Darwin himself is not altogether free, is that the deductive argument which is the core of the theory proves some sort of law of progressive development. Thus he concludes the chapter on 'Instincts' with the sentence: 'Finally, it may not be a logical deduction, but to my imagination it is far more satisfactory to look at such instincts as the young cuckoo ejecting its foster-brothers, — ants making slaves, — the larvae of ichneumonidae feeding within the live bodies of caterpillars, — not as specially endowed or created instincts, but as small consequences of one general law leading to the advancement of all organic beings, — namely, multiply, vary, let the strongest live and the weakest die.' Again in the penultimate paragraph of the whole book, he writes: 'As all the living forms of life are the lineal descendants of those which lived long before the Cambrian epoch, we may feel certain that . . . no cataclysm has desolated the whole world. Hence we may look with some confidence to a secure future of great length. And as natural selection works solely by and for the good of each being, all corporeal and mental endowments will tend to progress towards perfection.'[38]

The first of these two passages is not, perhaps, as clear and explicit as one could wish. But in the light of the unhesitating concluding sentence of the second we may perhaps take it that 'what may not be a logical deduction' is not 'the one general law leading to the advancement of all organic beings', but rather its suggested implications as regards the more unattractive instincts. Certainly Darwin is offering natural selection as a guarantee of progress, and as both a descriptive and a prescriptive law. Equally certainly this guarantee is not in fact warranted by his theory. Indeed, neither of the conclusions of the second passage can be justified as deductions from the theory alone.

The first was on the evidence available to Darwin an entirely reasonable inductive extrapolation. It is only since the beginning of the atomic era that we have acquired any serious grounds for anxiety about the immediate survival prospects for our own species. The second conclusion never was justified. To choose is necessarily to exclude, and there would seem to be no reason at all, and certainly none within the theory, for saying of every individual organism which loses out in the struggle for existence that this must be for its own good. Applied not to individuals but to species of beings, the statement might seem to find some justification in the now notorious fact that most actual variations are unfavourable. But since survival is in the theory the criterion of fitness, and hence of what counts as favourable, the only good which is guaranteed is the survival of whatever makes for survival; and this good is not necessarily good by any independent standard. Nor, of course, does natural selection guarantee that any particular species, or even any species at all, will enjoy even this purely biological good of having what it takes to survive.

Again, while presumably it does follow that, all other things being equal, the more efficient, and in that sense the more perfect, forms of any advantageous organ will tend to replace the less perfect forms, this is only guaranteed in so far as the organ in question does at the crucial times confer some decisive selective advantage upon the organism of which it is a part, and in so far as efficiency is defined in terms of survival value in that particular context. This more cautious and more correct formulation leaves open various discouraging possibilities, all of which would have to be disposed of before it could be allowed that the second of the present conclusions is warranted by the theory. This latter conclusion, it must be stressed, is much stronger than the first. Whereas that involved only a modestly confident extrapolation of an immemorial trend, this purports to find a theoretical basis for a boldly optimistic claim about a long-term tendency. The foundation is inadequate, for two reasons: first, because of the nature of the criterion of fitness which is involved in natural selection; and second, because that process operates on organisms and not on organs. Unless an organ is, directly or indirectly, relevant to the survival or the multiplication of the organism of which it is a part, natural selection will not engage with it at all; while an organism may labour under and be ruined by all sorts of other disadvantages which more than offset the selective promise of one particular organ. An individual, therefore, or a species can perfectly well have many splendid corporeal and mental endowments without this ensuring that it has what is in fact needed for survival: men who are wretched specimens, both mentally and physically, may — and all too often do — kill superb animals; and genius has frequently been laid low by the activities of unicellular creatures having no wits at all.

(iv) TRENDS, FORCES, AND LAWS OF DEVELOPMENT

Although it is thus wrong to think that Darwin's theory implies a general law of progressive development, the idea that it does has been and remains perennially tempting. Since it surely is the case that in every epoch of the fossil record fresh possibilities of life have been realised, since it also seems that the most complex of these in each epoch have been more elaborate than the most sophisticated achievements of the previous period, and since we ourselves are among the latest products of the development, it is easy to pick out a trend which we can scarcely regard as anything but progressive.

> . . . to have come so far,
> Whose cleverest invention was lately fur;
> Lizards my best once who took years to breed,
> Could not control the temperature of blood. . . .[39]

To pick out such a progressive trend is, of course, made still easier if we allow ourselves to misconstrue in a normative sense the palaeontologists' purely spatio-temporal use of the terms 'higher' and 'lower' to characterise first the strata and then the creatures whose fossils first appear in these strata. (It was not for nothing that Darwin pinned into his copy of *Vestiges of the Natural History of Creation* the memorandum slip: 'Never use the words *higher* and *lower*.'[40]

Once a trend has been thus identified it may seem a short step from a trend to the trend, another equally short from the trend to a law of tendency, and so again finally from a law of tendency to the universal overriding law of development. The slippery slope is greased by the facts that the crucial mechanism is called natural selection or the survival of the fittest, and that the core of Darwin's theory is a deductive argument which certainly does prove that natural selection is operating and is ensuring this survival of the fittest. But a trend is a very different thing from a law of tendency. There is a trend if there has been a direction in the development so far, whether or not there is any reason to think that things will continue to develop along this line. But to assert a law of tendency is to say that something always has occurred and always will occur, except in so far as this tendency was or will be inhibited by some overriding force. Furthermore, a law of tendency is a very different thing from an absolute law of development. The former may obtain even though the tendency in question is never in fact fully realised: the First Law of Motion and Malthus's Principle of Population are not disproved by the observations that in fact there always are 'impressed forces' and countervailing 'checks'.

But an absolute law of development would state that some particular line of evolution is absolutely inevitable, that it neither will nor could be prevented by any counteracting causes.

Darwin himself seems never to have gone further than to suggest, as in the two passages quoted, that his theory might warrant a law of the first and weaker kind — that there is in the evolution of all living things an inherent tendency to progress. It was left to others reviewing evolutionary biology in the light of their own various preconceptions about the destined lines of human development to discern in Darwinism the deeper foundation for or the wider background of their supposed absolute laws of human progress. By far the most interesting and most important case is that of Marx and Engels. In his Preface to the first German edition of *Capital* Marx writes: 'when a society has got upon the right track for the discovery of the natural laws of its movement — and it is the ultimate aim of this work to lay bare the economic law of motion of modern society — it can neither clear by bold leaps, nor remove by legal enactments, the obstacles offered by the successive phases of its normal development. But it can shorten and lessen the birth-pangs.' [41] And in his speech at Marx's graveside Engels claimed: 'Just as Darwin discovered the law of development of organic nature, so Marx discovered the law of development of human history.'

The crucial distinctions between actual trends, laws of tendency, and absolute laws of development can be illustrated from the writings of Julian Huxley and Joseph Needham; and the distinctions themselves are in turn essential to a proper critical appraisal of these writings. Thus Julian Huxley takes as one of the mottoes of his famous essay on 'Progress, Biological and Other' one of the sentences which we have just quoted from Darwin: 'As natural selection works solely by and for the good of each being, all corporeal and mental endowments will tend to progress towards perfection.' It is, I think, clear that Huxley if pressed would never claim to be showing more than a law of tendency, and usually only an actual trend.

He starts by urging that the most fundamental need of man as man is 'to discover something, some being or power, some force

21

or tendency . . . moulding the destinies of the world — something not himself, greater than himself, with which [he can] harmonise his nature . . . repose his doubts . . . achieve confidence and hope'. He then offers 'to show how the facts of evolutionary biology provide us, in the shape of a verifiable doctrine of progress, with one of the elements most essential to any such externally-grounded conception of God'. He later concludes that 'the fact of progress emerging from pain and battle and imperfection . . . is an intellectual prop which can support the distressed and questioning mind, and be incorporated into the common theology of the future'.[42]

All this would seem to require at least a law of tendency — a force — if not and preferably an invincible law of development. But in the intermediate small print Huxley attempts to establish only an actual trend, although he is later inclined to slip from this to the far stronger conclusion of a supporting tendency. Thus in that small print he claims: 'It will, I hope, have been clear, even from the few examples which I have given, that there has been a main direction in evolution.' He then defines this direction under six heads: 'During the time of life's existence on this planet, there has been an increase, both in the average and far more in the upper level, of certain attributes of living things.' However, in a concluding polemical paragraph against Dean Inge, Huxley both employs and neglects the distinction between such an actual trend and a supporting force: 'He has been so concerned to attack the dogma of inherent and inevitable progress in human affairs that he has denied the fact of progress — whether inevitable we know not, but indubitable and actual — in biological evolution: and in so doing he has cut off himself and his adherents . . . from by far the greatest manifestation in external things of "something, not ourselves, that makes for righteousness".'[43]

Although Huxley is certainly not adequately insistent upon the first crucial distinction between an actual trend and a force, he does in the following essay on 'Biology and Sociology' fairly clearly repudiate the suggestion that the actual progressive direction of development to be discerned in evolutionary biology and elsewhere necessarily reveals an absolute law of progressive development: 'When we look into the trend of biological evolution, we find as a matter of fact that it has operated to produce on the whole what we find good. . . . This is not to say that progress is an inevitable "law of nature", but that it has actually occurred. . . .'[44] This strongest idea of a law of inevitable development, rejected by Huxley, is in fact urged, eloquently and unequivocally, by Needham in two books of essays, *Time: the Refreshing River* and *History is on Our Side*. Generations which knew not the Spanish War may need to be told that the first of these titles is drawn from a stanza of Auden's since disowned 'Spain':

And the poor in their fireless lodgings, dropping the sheets
Of the evening paper: 'Our day is our loss, Oh, show us
History the operator, the
Organiser, Time the refreshing river.'[45]

It is worth quoting fairly extensively from these two Needham books, which are not as well known as they deserve to be, and which surely constitute both one of the most colourful and one of the most distinguished contributions to the often rather shabbily pedestrian corpus of evolutionary ethics and evolutionary politics. Much of their interest lies in the attempted synthesis of biological science, Marxist historical pseudo-science, and ritualistic Christian religion; the author was at the time of writing a leading biochemist, an active member of the Communist Party, and a practising Christian.

Thus Needham is able to write: 'The historical process is the organiser of the City of God, and those who work at its building are (in the old language) the ministers of the Most High . . . the curve of the development of human society pursues its way across the graph of history with statistical certainty . . .'; or 'the new world-order of social justice and comradeship, the rational and classless world state is no wild idealistic dream, but a logical extrapolation from the whole course of evolution, having no less authority than that behind it, and therefore of all faiths the most rational'; or 'the organisation of human society is only as yet at the beginning of its triumphs, and . . . these triumphs are *inevitable*, since they lie along the road traced out by the entire evolutionary process. . . .' (A footnote quotes the *Communist Manifesto*: 'The downfall of the bourgeoisie and the victory of the proletariat are equally *inevitable*.' [46]) Again, in the second book Needham urges: 'Whatever force hinders the coming of the world co-operative commonwealth . . . that force is ultimately doomed. Against the world-process no force can in the end succeed.' [47]

(v) LAWS AND INEVITABILITY

We have already argued, earlier in the present Section, that Darwin's theory does not provide a foundation adequate to sustain a general law of progress (III (iii) above); notwithstanding that it certainly is possible to pick out from the record of biological evolution so far trends which we human beings could scarcely fail to rate as progressive (III (iv) above). There is, therefore, no call for any further argument here to show that no absolute law of progressive development, which must as such be much stronger than any mere law of tendency, can possibly be derived from that theory; and, of course, there can be no question of deriving directly any sort of law at all from the observation only of an actual trend in the developments to date.

However, it is perhaps worth pointing out parenthetically that the spokesman for absolute laws of historical development must have difficulty in allowing room for effective human action; for, in so far as anything is absolutely inevitable, it would seem that attempts to prevent it must be futile and efforts to bring it about redundant; and this consequence is fatalism. It is this difficulty with which Marx — who had no wish whatsoever to become a 'remote and ineffectual don' — was trying to deal by introducing the idea of shortening and lessening the birthpangs; and which Needham — characteristically drawing on both the Chinese sages and Mr. R. Palme Dutt — tries to meet rather more fully.[48]

The line of approach actually taken here by Marx is importantly different from that of Needham and Palme Dutt. For, in effect, Marx is providing some — surely rather limited — scope for effective human action only by conceding that his law of development is imprecise. Development through the successive phases is in-

24

evitable and hence, it might seem, independent of any human wishes and decisions, although the speed, and the roughness or the smoothness, of this development can be affected by human choice. Palme Dutt on the other hand — and here he is perhaps being more faithful to the spirit and intentions of Marx than Marx himself — insists that all history is made by men, and hence that its course is always the outcome of human choices: 'It is the very heart of the revolutionary Marxist understanding of inevitability that it has nothing in common with the mechanical fatalism of which our opponents incorrectly accuse us. This inevitability is realised in practice through living human wills under given social conditions, consciously reacting to those conditions, and consciously choosing their line between alternative possibilities seen by them within the given conditions.'[49]

But now in so far as this is allowed it becomes thoroughly misleading to talk of any outcome as, without qualification, inevitable. For to say that something is, without qualification, inevitable is, surely, to imply that it is going to happen quite regardless and quite independent of any or all human decisions and human efforts; whereas Dutt's point is the entirely different one that, knowing — thanks to our Marxist analyses — what the situation is going to be and knowing too what people are like, we are entitled to be sure that they will react in ways which will effect such and such an outcome. Thus he continues: 'We are able scientifically to predict the inevitable outcome, because we are able to analyse the social conditions. . . . We are able to analyse the growth of contradictions, and the consequent . . . ever greater revolutionary consciousness and will in the exploited majority, till they become strong enough to overcome all obstacles and conquer. . . . But the human consciousness of the participants . . . is the consciousness of living, active, human beings, revolting against intolerable evils, deliberately with thought and passion choosing a new alternative, doing and daring all to achieve a new world. . . .'

The crux lies in the misplacement of the word 'inevitable'. It is one thing to say that, granted various truths or alleged truths about certain people and the situations in which they find themselves, then it necessarily follows that they will in fact act in such and such a way, and that the outcome will in fact be thus and thus. It is a very different thing to say that, granted these same truths or alleged truths, then the persons concerned will inevitably act in such and such a way, and that the inevitable outcome will be thus and thus. The point is that in the first case the necessity is logical, belonging only to the inference: here any 'inevitably' can qualify only the word 'follows', which links the premise propositions to the conclusion proposition. But in the second case the word 'inevitably' appears within the conclusion itself; and there it must carry a totally different, an empirical, sense. If the outcome is, without qualification, inevitable, then there can be nothing which anyone at all could do or could have done which would have prevented or would prevent that inevitable outcome. In a sentence: from 'Whatever will be will be' it follows necessarily that 'Whatever will be will be'; but it does not follow at all that 'Whatever will in fact be will have been inevitable'.[50]

One word more on Marxism and inevitability, before we return to Julian Huxley and his search for 'an intellectual prop which can support the distressed and questioning mind, and be incorporated in the common theology of the future'. It seems that Marxists, or at least those of the Muscovite obedience, are now inclined to abandon any idea of an absolute law of development towards a world socialist commonwealth, and instead to fall back on much weaker but still very strong laws of tendency. Thus the present writer was recently assured by the leading Marxist theoretician in Poland, himself a member of the Central Committee of the ruling Party, that socialism in one form or another was on its way — unless of course an all-out nuclear war produced universal ruin. Again, in England the Marxist philosopher Mr. Maurice Cornforth is now both stressing this same proviso and insisting — obviously rightly — that the defeat of the Axis powers in the Second World War was by no means inevitable.[51] If the point which we have just been making is accepted, this development will have to be characterised as a sensible shift: from the claim that, given a full Marxist understanding of man and society, we can know that the old original Clause 4 of the British

Labour Party will inexorably become the basic law for all mankind; to the rather more cautious contention that, granted that same understanding duly revised to take account of the facts of a new age, we can know that this supreme consummation will be effected unless a global nuclear catastrophe intervenes. In place of (what at any rate often looked like) an absolute law of development we now have (what quite clearly is) only a very strong law of tendency. All roads may still lead in the direction of socialism; but arrival at this destination is no longer so absolutely guaranteed.

(vi) EVOLUTION NOT 'SOMETHING, NOT OURSELVES, WHICH MAKES FOR RIGHTEOUSNESS'

The immediate relevance of all this to us here lies in its indirect bearing on hopes, such as we have seen expressed by Julian Huxley, of finding in evolutionary biology some sort of 'intellectual prop which can support the distressed and questioning mind'; or, more boldly, in the words of the definition of the moral function of God which Huxley quotes from Matthew Arnold, the hopes of finding 'something, not ourselves, that makes for righteousness'. There is a fundamental reason, which has so far been no more than hinted, why it must be misguided to seek such support in pre-human evolutionary biology alone, and without any special and particular reference to the peculiarities of the period of man. One hint lay in the contrast, which we developed early in this present Section, between natural selection and selection (III (ii) above). Ordinary literal selection always involves rational agents whereas natural selection typically does not. Another hint is to be found in our reasons for challenging Darwin's perhaps too optimistic presumption that 'we may look with some confidence to a secure future of great length'. Such confidence would be inductively justified only if we could discount the impact of man within the evolutionary process; only, it might therefore seem and paradoxically, if we were not here to be looking forward to anything at all.

The crux is, simply, that the future not only of mankind but of the entire evolutionary process on this planet is in our hands. The point is made with salutary brutality by Mr. A. M. Quinton, writing on 'Ethics and the Theory of Evolution'. He first notices how confidence in the possibility of discerning a progressive trend in the course of evolution so far 'seems to be based on the general agreement amongst biologists about the ordering of the evolutionary hierarchy'. He then remarks: 'One feature . . . which might be used is the unanimous opinion that man is the most evolved species, the one which shows the highest degree of biological progress. He has certainly won the contest between animal species in that it is only on his sufferance that any other species exist at all, amongst species large enough to be seen at any rate.' [52]

The same points are involved when Huxley himself, writing thirty years after his *Essays of a Biologist*, claims with visionary eloquence: 'In the light of evolutionary biology man can now see himself as the sole agent for further evolutionary advance on this planet, and one of the few possible instruments of progress in the universe at large. He finds himself in the unexpected position of business manager for the cosmic process of evolution.' [53]

We shall be considering in a later section this idea of seeing human life in an evolutionary perspective, an idea which becomes more and more prominent in Huxley's later essays (Section V below). But here the important thing to get clear is that, precisely in so far as it is true that the future both of mankind and of the entire evolutionary process on this planet — indeed in the whole solar system — is in our hands, to that extent there can be no question of finding any guarantee of future progress, either in the actual course of evolution before the emergence of man, or in its hypothetical development supposing there were to be no further human participation.

In the previous subsection we were insisting that men make history (III (v) above). One relevant consequence of this is that any predictions or assurances about the future course of that history require to be founded upon investigations of human nature and human society in particular, rather than upon a study of (prehuman) organic evolution in general. This is something which Marxists have always recognised: ' Just as Darwin discovered the law of organic nature, so Marx discovered the law of development of human history'; but each made his own discovery by enquiring in the appropriate area. Again, and typically, the dominant theme of Dr. John Lewis's *Man and Evolution* is the enormous difference between modern man and the other animals; and hence the equally enormous difference between human and pre-human evolution. Needham, because of his frank concern to retain some form of Christian belief, however Modernist, is atypical; yet he too insists repeatedly that the universal and progressive world-process proceeds through successive integrative levels each of which has its own laws requiring direct and independent study.[54]

The further point which we are now making is that not only do men make history — with the implication just indicated — but that the future course of the evolution of all other species is, or soon will be, in human hands — with the further implication that any substantial and particular predictions about developments there need also to take account of the peculiar powers and proclivities of our unique, and uniquely destructive, species.

The upshot of the present subsection is that the kind of reinforcement or guarantee sought by the author of *Essays of a Biologist* could be found only either 'outside' the universe, in an old-fashioned Divine Providence, or 'inside' the universe, in absolute laws of historical development. If the former could somehow be discovered then it would, presumably, follow that the course of biological evolution up to and including the emergence of man must have been — like everything else in the universe — a manifestation of that Divine Providence; and that, presumably, must imply that all manner of things are and were and will be well. Again, if there were absolute laws of historical development, and if the development which they determined could be rated as progressive, then Huxley might have found in these laws that outside support which he craved. (It would be outside support — 'something, not ourselves' — since it is an essential feature of any such Juggernaut view of history that any development determined by its absolute laws is altogether outside human control. Precisely that is what makes the Juggernaut a Juggernaut; and it is this feature which makes Popper's phrase 'the Juggernaut view of history' apt.)

But either recourse ought to be suspect in a supposedly secular context. There is, surely, something very odd, indeed pathetic, in Huxley's attempt to find in evolutionary biology 'something, not ourselves, which makes for righteousness'. For this quest is for him a search for something, not God, which does duty for Divine Providence. Yet if there really is no Divine Providence operating in the universe, then indeed there is none; and we cannot reasonably expect to find in the Godless workings of impersonal things those comfortable supports which — however mistakenly — believers usually think themselves entitled to derive from their theistic beliefs. Nor, in so far as we insist — as indeed we must — that men make history, can any laws of tendency which we may be able to discover in history fill Huxley's bill. For, in so far as such laws either epitomise or presuppose our human tendencies, they very obviously cannot, whether or not they make for righteousness, constitute a 'something, not ourselves'.

There cannot, therefore, be the answer longed for to the heart-cry: 'Oh, show us / History the operator, the / Organiser . . .'. Still less is there any profit in our

> . . . invoking the life
> That shapes the individual belly and orders
> The private nocturnal terror:
> 'Did you not found the city state of the sponge
>
> Raise the vast military empires of the shark
> And the tiger, establish the robin's plucky canton?
> Intervene . . .'

No doubt it is in part because Auden himself now hopes that there is, after all, someone who might 'descend as a dove or / A furious papa or a mild engineer, but descend', that he has become so averse from any reprinting of 'Spain'. Nevertheless, the author's own backslidings notwithstanding, the final stanza is the last word on the early Huxley's hopes:

> The stars are dead. The animals will not look.
> We are left alone with our day, and the time is short, and
> History to the defeated
> May say Alas but cannot help nor pardon.[55]

IV. FROM *IS* TO *OUGHT*

The panorama presented by evolutionary biology is, though often terrible, magnificent; and to have brought the development of all living things within the scope of a single theory constitutes one of the greatest achievements of the human mind. 'Thus', in the concluding words of the *Origin*, 'from the war of nature, from famine and death, the most exalted object which we are capable of conceiving, namely, the production of the higher animals, directly follows. There is grandeur in this view of life, with its several powers originally breathed by its Creator into a few forms or into one; and that, whilst this planet has gone cycling on according to the fixed law of gravity, from so simple a beginning endless forms most beautiful and most wonderful have been, and are being evolved.'[56] There is indeed.

It is, therefore, as we insisted at the very beginning, neither surprising nor discreditable that people should want to adjust their ideas to this vision, and to seek possible wider applications for the concepts of evolutionary theory. In the previous section we considered one kind of suggestion about 'the philosophical implications of Darwinism'. In the present section we shall run through some major variations on the theme of the Naturalistic Fallacy. This has certainly been central in much which has been called evolutionary ethics; so much so that it has often, but wrongly, been thought to be the essential and polymorphous error which must both constitute and vitiate everything so labelled.

(i) A SPECIAL CASE

The first move is to distinguish what is peculiar to one special case from what is common to all such attempted deductions. Their general character, as has been indicated already, is determined by the fact that all the premises are, or should be, purely descriptive;

31

whereas the conclusions obtained are to be taken as prescriptive. The peculiarity of the special case is that here the premises are universal propositions the truth of which is dependent upon their being consistent with the facts that we do do whatever it may be that we do actually do. But it must be radically preposterous, not but what it has been and is common, to try to generate some mandate to do this rather than that from propositions which, to be truly what they pretend to be, must either be equally consistent with the choice of either alternative or be wholly inconsistent with our having any alternatives at all. It would be idle and absurd to seek prescriptions for our behaviour where we are not confronted with options for choice, and unless the prescriptions sought are to require some of these and to forbid others.

We have already noticed one instance of the special case (III (i) above). We also, later in that Section (III (v) above), approached from a rather different direction the presently crucial point. D. G. Ritchie was there quoted as trying to rebut the policy of prudential restraint urged by Malthus, by urging that this must lead to 'the survival of the unfittest'. Yet this is a conclusion which must be, in Darwinian terms, contradictory. For survival, or — strictly — survival to reproduce, is not the reward but the criterion of biological fitness. But, of course, in so far as we maintain — and rightly — some standard of human excellence other than mere reproduction or multiplication, there may indeed be all too much reason for us to fear and deplore the present and likely future outcome of high reproductive rates among the backward, the improvident, and the fanatical.

Further examples of what we are distinguishing as the special case can be generated wherever we have what is supposed to be a law of nature including human action within its scope. For if it really is a law of nature, then it follows that nothing which has happened, is happening, or will happen can be inconsistent with it; any occurrence inconsistent with it constitutes a sufficient reason for disallowing its claim to express a law of nature. There is, therefore, a further special absurdity — over and above whatever general fallacy may be involved in any attempt to deduce normative conclusions from neutrally descriptive premises — in appealing to a premise of this sort as if, simultaneously, it could both express such a law of nature and constitute a reason for acting in one way rather than another.

The crux can be illustrated, light-heartedly but very aptly, by referring to a crisp exchange recorded in Mr. Raymond Chandler's *Farewell, My Lovely*. Philip Marlowe is conversing with Anne Riordan: "You take awful chances, Miss Riordan." "I think I said the same about you. I had a gun. I wasn't afraid. There's no law against going down there." "Uh-huh. Only the law of self-preservation." With his accustomed acuteness Marlowe, returning the gun, corrects himself: "Here. It's not my night to be clever."[57] Certainly, interpreted as other than a wisecrack, his remark would be foolish. For, precisely in so far as there were a psychological law of self-preservation under which all our actual actions could be subsumed, there could be no point in appealing to this law as a reason for acting not in one way but another; while if after all no such law holds, then it cannot provide any reasonable ground for anything. All those who in martyrdom witness to their conviction that survival can sometimes be too dearly bought do not thereby rebel against Nature's law of self-preservation. Rather they demonstrate that no such law obtains; or, at any rate, that if it does, the human animal does not fall within its scope.

Various misunderstandings of and ambiguities in the key terms and expressions have in the Darwinian context helped to conceal this absurdity; notwithstanding that, as we suggested in the Introduction, the great diversity and the frequent mutual inconsistency of the practical morals actually drawn ought surely to have made the supposed method of derivation suspect. Since the major misunderstandings and ambiguities have been noticed already in passing, we need here only to review them and to provide further illustrations.

First, and certainly not confined to our present biological context, is the failure to distinguish two kinds of law of nature — or, better, two senses of 'law of nature': the descriptive, in which such a law cannot have any genuine exceptions, since the occurrence of any event inconsistent with the truth of a proposed law constitutes a sufficient reason for failing the candidate; and the prescriptive, in which the occurrence of violations constitutes no reason at all for maintaining that the law originally propounded does not really obtain. The point of the passage just quoted from *Farewell, My Lovely* lies in its wisecracking exploitation of this ambiguity. But, as is shown by other examples which we have given and shall give, the fact that one can draw an illustration from such a source must be interpreted not as evidence of the universal obviousness of the crucial distinction but as one more indication of the quality of Chandler.

Second, the expression 'natural selection' seems to be used in two crucially different senses: both, more narrowly, in an incompatible contrast with '(artificial) selection' and, comprehensively, in such a way that the latter is just a special case of the former. It becomes absolutely essential to make this distinction the moment we wish to take account of the actual or possible impact of human choice upon the course of biological evolution. We have already tried, in the previous Section (III (vi) above), to show how the past, present, and potential impact of our own species upon and within this development rules out any possibility of discovering at the sub-human levels some comfortably reassuring substitute for Divine Providence. We can now appreciate, in the light of everything which has been said in this present subsection, why it is even more fundamentally misguided to hope to make a law of natural selection into the arbiter or the scapegoat on to which we can shuffle off the burdens of human decision and human responsibility. For in so far as the law applies to us at all it can only be because 'natural selection' is being construed in the comprehensive second sense in which there can be no antithesis between natural and artificial selection, because whatever we do in fact select is by that token shown to have been selected naturally.

With all the advantages of hindsight we may well regret that Darwin himself did not in the *Origin* explicitly make, and make much of, this distinction between a narrower and a wider sense of 'natural selection'. But it is much more regrettable, and far less excusable, that a writer on *Darwin and the Darwinian Revolution* now, a full century later, should still fail altogether to seize the points involved. Thus we read that: 'Francis Galton, Darwin's cousin and great champion, who made it his mission, as he thought, to give practical content to Darwin's theory, was by this very enterprise denying that theory. The science of eugenics, devoted to the improvement of the human stock, was designed "to further the ends of evolution more rapidly and with less distress than if events were left to their own course".' Darwin's own sympathetic yet pessimistic reactions to one of Galton's eugenic proposals are then mentioned, and the occasion grasped to rebuke poor Darwin because 'It did not seem to have occurred to him that it vitiated his essential principle, making survival independent of the natural struggle for existence.'[58] On this scandalous bit of commentary we may comment in turn, equally superciliously but with justification, that it does not seem to have occurred to the authoress that a programme for the improvement — by reference, presumably, to some human standards of excellence and fitness — of our own human stock could be no more and no less inconsistent with Darwin's theory than are the activities of those throughout the centuries who have selected for desired varieties of plants and animals and against others — activities to which he himself gave the most careful attention in the first chapter of the *Origin*, and elsewhere.

Third, the two logically connected expressions 'natural selection' and 'survival of the fittest' are within the theory implicitly so defined that whatever is in fact 'selected' and survives must necessarily be the fittest, regardless of all other merits or demerits, and notwithstanding that both expressions contain terms which are often or always elsewhere employed for commendation (III (i) above). Granted this Darwinian criterion of fitness it becomes a necessary truth that whatever survives to reproduce is fit, and must have been naturally selected; although this, it is just worth reiterating, does not imply, what is not true, that to say that natural selection occurs is to utter a tautology.[59] When a failure to take account of the difference between the Darwinian and other more ordinary criteria of fitness for selection is combined with a blindness to the equivocation between two senses of 'law', it becomes easy, first to misplace the idea of necessity, and then to misconstrue it. A logical necessity is thus unwittingly transmogrified into, and hence appears to reinforce, a moral necessity: compare the way in which, as we have seen (III (v) above), the logical necessity of an implication may be alchemically transmuted into the practical inevitability of an event. To say within the terms of Darwinian theory that in natural selection the fittest must survive is to utter only a tautology. But this can be mistaken to be an urgent practical imperative, categorically demanding that we make every sacrifice to ensure that they in fact do.

Thus — to go straight to the bottom — consider the savage 'Social Darwinism' which Adolf Hitler assimilated in the Vienna of his youth: 'If we did not respect the law of nature, imposing our will by the right of the stronger, a day would come when the wild animals would again devour us — then the insects would eat the wild animals, and finally nothing would exist on earth except the microbes'; or again, 'By means of the struggle the élites are continually renewed. The law of selection justifies this incessant struggle by allowing the survival of the fittest. Christianity is a rebellion against natural law, a protest against nature. Taken to its logical extreme Christianity would mean the systematic cult of human failure.'[60]

These passages from an outrageous source very effectively underline the present point: actual survival to reproduce is itself within Darwin's theory the sole and sufficient criterion of fitness thus to survive; and the mere capacity to survive and to reproduce is the only and often humanly very questionable merit for which natural selection necessarily selects. An 'élite' selected simply on this basis could be, literally as well as metaphorically, the scum which rises to the top. But the same passages also illustrate the crucial confusions between the two senses of 'law' and the two senses of 'natural selection'. The anti-Christian moral which Hitler draws may be salutarily compared with Rockefeller's Sunday-school claim, quoted already in our Introduction: 'The growth of a large business is merely a survival of the fittest. . . . This is not an evil tendency in business. It is merely the working out of a law of nature and a law of God.'

We end this subsection with two further illustrations: one to show that the same misconceptions have been accepted by more disinterested protagonists, the other to reveal that a first-rate philosopher is not necessarily immune. First, from the founder and first General of the Salvation Army: 'In the struggle of life the weakest will go to the wall and there are so many weak. The fittest, in tooth and claw, will survive. All we can do is to soften the lot of the unfit and make their sufferings less horrible than at present.'[61] Although we have provided already all the instruments required for the dissection, it is perhaps just worth adding that many of those who, by Booth's human and humane criteria, scored as the weakest who went to the wall would, by the biological criterion of mere survival to multiply, not have counted as weak at all. For in Booth's day as today high fertility was often both a cause and a consequence of poverty.

Second, from C. S. Peirce: '*The Origin of Species* of Darwin merely extends politico-economical views of progress to the entire realm of animal and vegetable life. . . . As Darwin puts it on his title page, it is the struggle for existence; and he should have added for his motto: "Every individual for himself, and the Devil take the hindmost!" Jesus, in his Sermon on the Mount, expressed a different opinion.' Peirce goes on to tell us that 'The Gospel of Christ says that progress comes from every individual merging his individuality in sympathy with his neighbours', and Peirce contrasts this with what 'may accurately be called the Gospel of Greed'. It was not one of Peirce's good days, for only a page or two later, in the same article, on 'Evolutionary Love', he says: 'Another thing: anaesthetics had been [in 1859] in use for thirteen years. Already, people's acquaintance with suffering had dropped off very much; and, as a consequence, that unlovely hardness, by which our times are so contrasted with those that immediately preceded them, had already set in and inclined people to relish a ruthless theory.'[62]

(ii) THE NATURALISTIC FALLACY AS SUCH

In (i) above, although most of our distinctions and arguments had some wider application, we were primarily concerned with one special case of the attempt to deduce normative conclusions from the purely descriptive premises provided by evolutionary theory. We now proceed to consider the Naturalistic Fallacy in general, although always of course with special reference to its application in our context. The label 'Naturalistic Fallacy' derives from G. E. Moore's *Principia Ethica* (1903). It is an apt label, since one very typical way of committing this fallacy is by offering some supposedly neutral descriptive statement about what is allegedly natural as if it could by itself entail some conclusion about what is in some way commendable. Yet Moore's own account is so wrapped up in various unfortunate assumptions that — all other reasons apart — it is wise to begin from the now much-quoted passage from Hume, noting by the way that *Principia Ethica* neither quotes nor mentions this earlier classical authority.

Hume presents his remarks as an important afterthought to the first Section of Book iii of his *Treatise of Human Nature* (1740), under the section title 'Moral Distinctions not Derived from Reason': 'In every system of morality which I have hitherto met with I have always remarked that the author proceeds for some time in the ordinary way of reasoning, and establishes the being of a God, or makes observations concerning human affairs; when of a sudden I am surprised to find, that instead of the usual copulations of propositions, *is* and *is not*, I meet with no proposition that is not connected with an *ought* or *ought not*. This change is imperceptible; but is, however, of the last consequence. For as this *ought* or *ought not* expresses some new relation or affirmation, it is necessary that it should be observed and explained; and at the same time a reason should be given, for what seems altogether inconceivable, how this new relation can be a deduction from others, which are entirely different from it.'

This observation is so important — and one is tempted to add, mischievously, so clear and so clearly sound — that there is now no lack of well-girded champions eager to contest both its accepted interpretation and its truth. We can here eschew most of the details of Hume scholarship, doing so the less reluctantly for having ourselves participated vigorously in the recent discussion in the journals.[63] Yet it is relevant to our present purposes to warn the unwary not to be misled by Hume's irony. It would be completely wrong to take him absolutely literally, as if he were modestly claiming only to have noticed, and to have become seized of the vast importance of, a distinction which, however unwittingly, everyone was always and systematically making already. If that really had been Hume's contention it would, of course, have been quite obviously false, and could have been disposed of even more briskly than some of his most impatient critics have thought to be rid of it.[64]

However, Hume was not that — or any — sort of a fool. His immediate thesis was not that a distinction always is made, and that it is invariably marked by those different copulations of propositions, *ought* and *is*; but rather that it always ought to be made, because it is 'of the last consequence'. And why it is of the last consequence is, in Hume's view, that it is an expression and an implication of what he thought to be the great fundamental truth — and one of his own prime insights in philosophy — that values are not any sort of property of things in themselves, but that they are in some way a projection out on to the things around us of human needs and human desires. (One resulting problem, more obvious perhaps to us than to Hume, is that of explaining how values can be in some such fundamental way dependent on, and some sort of function of, human needs and human desires, without its thereby becoming the case that some purely descriptive statements about what people do want or would want must entail consequences about what ought to be. It is more than enough here for us simply to notice this problem, and to remark that it is at least not obvious that Hume completely forgot his point of the last consequence when he came to give his positive accounts of morals and aesthetics.)

Once Hume's ostensibly afterthought observation is understood, the first question is whether such a distinction, with a logical Grand Canyon between its terms, really can be made and maintained. It must be entirely beside the point to preen oneself — as some have done — upon having rustled up a herd of words which combine elements of both sorts in their meanings, or of expressions which can be ambiguous as between one and the other. For what has to be shown is not that this basic distinction is not in fact always made, but that in principle it cannot be.

Another recent approach calls attention to a 'class of unquestionably descriptive practical statements, namely what I shall call *appetitive utterances*, which indicate the objects or states of affairs that the person addressed will most enjoy or like or will get most satisfaction from. "You will most like or enjoy the Red Lion" is as good, sufficient and direct an answer to the question "Which hotel shall I stay at?" as "Stay at the Red Lion" or "The Red Lion is the best hotel". It is like them and different from "The Red Lion is the smartest or largest or quietest hotel" in that no contingent presumption needs to be made about the special tastes or requirements of the questioner in order to predict the action that will follow on his sincere acceptance of the advice, or at any rate to be assured of its relevance to his enquiry.' [65]

Yet neither that you would most enjoy the Red Lion, nor that it is the best hotel, constitutes an indefeasibly good reason for your staying there. You may, for instance, not be able or willing to afford the best, just as you may have some special reason, moral or other, which forbids indulgence on this (or any other) occasion. What is special about these appetitive utterances is, not that they make no contingent presumption about the requirements of the person addressed, but that the presumption involved is in fact almost always correct. But even if it were correct, not just usually but absolutely invariably, the conclusion to be derived from any appetitive premise would still be purely factual: if it is enjoyment you are after — as in fact, like everybody else, you are — then this is what in this particular case will serve your turn. So the subsistence of appetitive truths seems to have in itself no tendency to show that an *ought* can, after all, be deduced from an *is*.

A third and very plausible approach — persuasively suggested within the present series by Mr. G. J. Warnock in sections v and vi of his *Contemporary Moral Philosophy* — urges that at least part of what distinguishes moral ideals and moral values from ideals and values of other sorts is that morality is always supposed to be directed towards the welfare of those concerned. Now if this is indeed so, and assuming that no one's welfare could be consistent with the wholesale frustration of all his desires, it might seem that one should be able to deduce some moral conclusions from some collections of flawlessly factual premises about what is or would be desired. Certainly from premises about what people want we can hope to deduce conclusions about what would satisfy or frustrate them; while equally certainly we can, if we like, characterise the promotion of their satisfaction as moral. Such a characterisation can probably be justified both by an appeal to (much of) the common usage of the term 'moral' and its associates, and also by reference to the point and purpose of moral discourse. Yet no such attempt, however successful, to construe 'moral' in terms of what is or would be desired by any individual or group could even begin to show that we can validly deduce, from the proposition that something is in this way and by these persons desired, the totally different conclusion that it is indeed desirable (in the sense of being what ought to be desired). For the crucial difference will still warrant the crucial distinction: between, on the one hand, simply stating quite neutrally that these are the things which would satisfy such and such desires; and, on the other hand, going on to prescribe that these particular desires are desires which ought to be satisfied.

However, the present occasion no more demands an exhaustive defence of Hume's thesis in its accepted interpretation than it calls for an attempt to show that that interpretation embodies the correct reading of Hume; and here again we can disclaim the task with a better conscience for having already taken a part in discussion in the journals. The main reason for making those remarks which we have made is further to clarify what the Naturalistic Fallacy is supposed to be, before proceeding to examine some particular moves — moves which can be seen to be fallacious without the support of any fully worked-out and impregnably defended general characterisation; and yet moves the unsoundness of which will need somehow to be taken into account by those philosophers who propose to deny that the Naturalistic Fallacy is a fallacy. The need to allow for this should give pause; as, in another way, should the recognition that though the label was a philosopher's coinage the idea itself is not peculiar to our notoriously fallible and perverse profession. Einstein, for instance, took it as obvious that 'As long as we remain within the realm of science proper, we can never meet with a sentence of the type "Thou shalt not kill". . . . Scientific statements of facts and relations . . . cannot produce ethical directives'.[66]

When we come to particular cases the most notable thing is precisely the lack of precision as to what the connection between the biological facts and the ethical directives is supposed to be. For instance, Julian Huxley tells us that 'in the broadest possible terms evolutionary ethics must be based on a combination of a few main principles: that it is right to realise ever new possibilities in evolution, notably those which are valued for their own sake; that it is right both to respect human individuality and to encourage its fullest development; that it is right to construct a mechanism for further social evolution which shall satisfy these prior conditions as fully, efficiently, and rapidly as possible.'[67]

It would be hard to dispute either that this is a statement 'in the broadest possible terms', or — as he goes on to say — that 'to translate these arid-sounding generalities into concrete terms and satisfying forms is beyond the scope of a lecture'. Again, after our earlier stress on the enormous difference between saying that something is desired and saying that it is desirable, we are bound to notice the tendency to equate the valuable with what is in fact valued: 'that it is right to realise ever new possibilities in evolution, notably those which are valued for their own sake'. But it is not necessarily an objection, although it is no doubt true, to say that the directives indicated seem in no way distinctively evolutionary. Certainly they might have been — indeed they often were and are — accepted without benefit of Darwin. Yet the claim to be propounding an evolutionary ethics might still have been abundantly vindicated if only Huxley had spelt out, as he never did, the steps of the logical deduction which, as 'the evolutionary moralist', he maintained was possible: 'He [the evolutionary moralist] can tell us that the facts of nature, as demonstrated in evolution, give us the assurance that knowledge, love, beauty, selfless morality, and firm purpose are ethically good.'[68] Well, no doubt he can tell us. But that, in default of any less elliptical exposition, is no sufficient reason for agreeing that what he tells us is true.

Again, if we turn to Spencer we find a similar indeterminacy about precisely what supposed evolutionary facts are to be connected with the desired ethical directives, and how; an indeterminacy which, in his case, cannot plausibly be excused by reference to any restriction of space. It is significant that in the Preface to the second heavy volume of *The Principles of Ethics* he is ready to concede that, in the last two parts, 'the Doctrine of Evolution . . . helps us in general ways though not in special ways'. But, even in a part to which this is supposed not to apply, a section which begins with the bold promise that 'Acceptance of the doctrine of organic evolution determines certain ethical conceptions' ends with only the unshattering and uncommunicative conclusion that it is 'an inevitable inference from the doctrine of organic evolution, that the highest type of living being, no less than all lower types, must go on moulding itself to those requirements which circumstances impose'.[69] One may perhaps recall here the statement which once introduced the lead story in an international news magazine notorious for the breathless urgency of its house style: 'Last week, as in every week in human history, in the best of times and in the worst of times, the leaders of the world's nations played out their separate parts.'

The proper objection to this is that it suffers not so much from a surfeit of generality as from a deficiency of substance. But there are other claims against which the same charge could not be laid. Consider three: first, 'that the conduct to which we apply the name *good*, is the relatively more evolved conduct; and *the bad* is the name which we apply to conduct which is relatively less evolved'; second, that 'no school can avoid taking for the ultimate moral aim a desirable state of feeling . . . gratification, enjoyment, happiness. Pleasure somewhere, at some time, to some being or beings, is an inexpugnable element of the conception'; and third, that 'the process of evolution must inevitably favour all changes of nature which increase life and augment happiness: especially such as do this at small cost'.[70]

Now, as we argued at length in Section III, Darwin's theory

43

provides no basis for concluding that there is any such law of progress as Spencer seems to be proclaiming in the third of these passages. Nor will it do to say, what the first passage seems to be suggesting, that moral behaviour is somehow more sophisticated biologically, or more a product of evolution, than immoral. For even if we allow 'the origin of the moral sentiments, in the same way as other natural phenomena, by a process of evolution', still 'as the immoral sentiments have no less been evolved, there is, so far, as much natural sanction for the one as for the other'.[71] The temptation, compounded by the strong suggestion of ordinary usage that any evolution must be from the inferior to the superior, is to mistake it that evolution in the Darwinian context must be ever towards more and better. Then, conjoining this misconception with the second less exceptionable claim, we bring forth the comfortable conclusion that the process of biological evolution must be a progress towards the supreme good of the classical Utilitarians, the greatest happiness of the greatest number.

In this argument, which can at best be a reconstruction of only one strand of Spencer's thinking, the conclusion is mediated by an ambiguity in 'evolution': between, on the one hand, the neutral scientific sense, and, on the other hand, a sense in which any evolution necessarily tends in a direction which must be rated as good. Even supposing, what we earlier urged is not and cannot be the case, that there really were some immanent guarantee that as a matter of contingent fact evolution in the former sense does produce these good results, still it must be quite wrong to try to equate the evolved with the good or the good with the evolved. The crucial point was made forcefully by Russell over fifty years ago, in words which read piquantly today: 'If evolutionary ethics were sound, we ought to be entirely indifferent as to what the course of evolution may be, since whatever it is is thereby proved to be the best. Yet if it should turn out that the Negro or the Chinaman was able to oust the European, we should cease to have any admiration for evolution; for as a matter of fact our preference of the European to the Negro is wholly independent of the European's greater prowess with the Maxim gun.'[72] And, it is fair to

44

add, the same could with the appropriate alterations be said of Russell's own present preference for the Chinese and the Vietcong.

Russell's argument is decisive against any attempt to define the ideas of right and wrong, good and evil, in terms of a neutrally scientific notion of evolution. It can, as we shall see, be equally effective against the rather different suggestion that Darwin's theory can supply us with a, or even with the, satisfactory moral criterion. But before moving on to that we must break a lance with the shrewd and scholarly author of *The Moral Theory of Evolutionary Naturalism*. For, notwithstanding that he himself notices and cites earlier and better formulations by Hume and others, what seems to be the main thesis of his book constitutes an instructive example of an ideologically important misconception encouraged by one of the peculiarities of Moore's treatment. This thesis is that 'in so far as the evolutionary moralists' treatment of ethical questions is naturalistic, it is not normative; and that in so far as normative considerations are introduced it is not naturalistic'. He refers, approvingly, to Guyau: 'Most Evolutionary Naturalists, he declares, have made the great mistake of giving a naturalistic account and "also pretending to have rendered it . . . imperative in its precepts".' [73] Quillian's conclusion is that by introducing the normative the evolutionary naturalists have tacitly acknowledged the inadequacy of a naturalistic world-view. [74]

To understand both why this should be thought and why it is mistaken it is necessary to go back first to Moore and then to Hume. Moore, as we have said, introduced the label 'Naturalistic Fallacy', but, as we also mentioned, he characterised the mistake in a most unfortunate manner (a way, incidentally, which would make it a mistake in introspective psychology and not in logic — and hence not, strictly speaking, a fallacy at all). It was for him the error of believing 'that when we think "This is good", what we are thinking is that the thing in question bears a definite relation to some one other thing'. But then immediately, and without perhaps fully appreciating the possibilities of confusion opened up by thus using the word 'naturalistic' both in a peculiar and also in a less peculiar sense, he goes on to distinguish two sorts of view: on the one hand, 'Naturalistic Ethics'; and, on the other,

'Metaphysical Ethics'. In Moore both equally are taken to involve the Naturalistic Fallacy. The former is distinguished by the fact that here the value words are implicitly or explicitly defined in terms of something natural. This too is duly explained: 'By "nature" . . . I mean . . . that which is the subject-matter of the natural sciences and also of psychology.'[75]

So far it might seem that Quillian had simply misread his Moore, however excusably. But Moore straightway proceeds to introduce a distinction between natural and non-natural properties, and asks: 'Which among the properties of natural objects are natural properties and which are not?' He insists that goodness — for Moore *good* is always the key term in ethics — is just such a non-natural characteristic: 'For I do not deny that good is a property of certain natural objects: certain of them, I think, *are* good.'[76] Now if this were all right, then there would be certain things in the universe possessing properties which must necessarily be beyond the range of 'the natural sciences and of psychology'. And if to introduce the normative is, as this suggests, tacitly to recognise the subsistence of such non-natural properties, then indeed the evolutionary naturalists — and everyone else too who does the same — is thereby implicitly acknowledging the inadequacy of a naturalistic world-view.

This shows how Quillian, by following Moore, could be led to think what he did. To appreciate why this thought is mistaken it is helpful to go back further still, to Hume. As everyone must know, it was Hume's ambition 'to introduce the experimental method of reasoning into moral subjects',[77] and thereby to effect a sort of Copernican revolution in reverse. For Hume the paradigm for this exercise was the achievement of the new optics, construed as showing that colours are not truly qualities of the things which we uninstructedly describe as coloured. Rather they are somehow projections from our own 'sensoria'.[78] It was in these terms that Hume would have us see 'that morality is nothing in the abstract nature of things, but is entirely relative to the sentiment or mental taste of each particular being, in the same manner as the distinctions of sweet and bitter, hot and cold arise from the particular feeling of each sense or organ'.[79]

46

But now if, as Hume suggests, putting a value on something or commending some course of action neither is nor presupposes the ascription of any supposed non-natural characteristics to anything, then there is no longer any reason for thinking that anyone who — as we all must — values, commends, recommends, prescribes, and so on, must thereby be — however unwittingly — acknowledging the existence of some reality of which a naturalistic world-outlook cannot take account. For except in so far as some Moorean account is correct, none of these proceedings seems to present any insuperable obstacle to tough-mindedly naturalistic description. Certainly many spokesmen of a naturalistic world-outlook, including most of Quillian's Evolutionary Naturalists, have also been, like many of their opponents, committers of the Naturalistic Fallacy. But there is no necessary connection between naturalism, in the sense in which the word refers to a sort of world-view, and naturalism, in the rather artificial sense in which a naturalist would be one who tried to deduce *ought*s from *is*es. Hume, for instance, and in this he was not inconsistent, was as surely a naturalist in the first sense as he was committed to rejecting naturalism in the second.

(iii) NOT THE MEANING BUT THE CRITERION?

In the previous subsection we considered the possibility of deducing ethical conclusions directly from premises supplied by evolutionary biology. For any such move to be sound the prescription in the conclusion must be somehow incapsulated in the premises; for, by definition, a valid deduction is one in which you could not assert the premises and deny the conclusion without thereby contradicting yourself. A more modest suggestion, not always properly distinguished as such, is that, although the present meanings of our moral words cannot be explicated either wholly or partly in evolutionary terms, still evolution somehow supplies a necessary criterion. This seems to be the view of, for instance, Needham. For he welcomes the 'expulsion of ethics from biology and embryology' and notes: 'That *good* and *bad*, *noble* and *ignoble*, *beautiful* and *ugly*, *honourable* and *dishonourable*, are not terms with a biological meaning is a proposition which it has taken many centuries for biologists to realise.' Nevertheless, elsewhere he urges: 'The evolutionary process itself supplies us with a criterion of the good.'[80]

Now, assuming that our reading is correct, this move involves no crude attempt to deduce a moral *ought* from an evolutionary *is*. But Needham is still exposed to Russell's objection: 'If evolutionary ethics were sound, we ought to be entirely indifferent as to what the course of evolution may be, since whatever it is it is thereby proved to be the best.' The decisiveness of this objection was no doubt concealed from Needham by two things: first, the by now familiar ambiguity in the word 'evolution' (IV (ii) above); and second, his own conviction that, as a matter of contingent fact, biological evolution has a direction which he was prepared to rate as progressive (III (iv) above). The shift from the neutral to a commendatory sense of 'evolution' is well illustrated in the paragraph from which our second quotation is taken: in that particular sentence the sense must be the former. But two or three sentences further on it is equally clearly the latter: 'The kind of behaviour which has furthered man's social evolution in the past can be seen very well by viewing human history; and the great ethical teachers, from Confucius onwards, have shown us . . . how men may live together in harmony, employing their several talents to the general good.'[81]

It might perhaps be suggested that Russell's point really would lose its force if once it were to be conceded that, as a matter of contingent fact, evolution is tending to move, and is perhaps actually moving, in a commendable direction. If only, it might be urged, this were to be conceded, then there could be no objection to adopting some evolutionary criterion of the good; and we might proceed to argue that 'when we have found our Ten Commandments in general evolution' we can go on to 'discover our *Deuteronomy* in political analysis'.[82]

The one grain of truth in the main suggestion is that anyone equipped with such a mixed factual-cum-evaluative premise would be in a position to make valid inferences from purely factual evolutionary premises to evaluative conclusions. But, precisely

48

because of the mixed character of this second premise, this must be without prejudice to anything so far said about inferences from purely factual premises to evaluative conclusions. What is not true in this suggestion is the heart of the matter, the idea that Russell's objection can be escaped by appealing to such a mixed premise. It cannot. For consider how the exchanges must go. The protagonist says that his criterion of the right is found in the actual direction of evolution. The deuteragonist replies that in that case the protagonist is committed to approving the direction of evolution quite regardless of what it may turn out to be. The latter then triumphantly appeals to his happy discovery that, as a matter of fact, the direction of evolution is as it ought to be. But now, on the protagonist's own chosen terms, this discovery must be wholly lacking in factual content. For, in so far as his criterion of the right lies in the actual direction of evolution, it becomes necessarily true that the actual direction is as it ought to be. The contingent fact to which the protagonist appealed thus disappears; but not before the very making of any such appeal has tacitly conceded Russell's point.

Waddington's striking employment of Biblical terms may usefully provoke the reflection that all the moves and counter-moves which we have been discussing here can be paralleled in discussions as to whether moral ideas can be defined in terms of the will of God, or whether — failing that — God's will could serve as an acceptable criterion of the right and the good. It might indeed even be urged that a main justification for going through all these moves and counter-moves at length here is as a training for recognising and dealing with mistakes of the same form made in other contexts.

Be that as it may, there certainly are some remarkable formal analogies between evolutionary ethics as expounded by Waddington and the arguments of those moral theologians who have tried to derive their often peculiarly clerical norms from the supposed intentions of nature: for instance, the argument — rather less frequently heard in the last year or two — that all 'artificial' contraception must be wrong because it involves a frustration of the natural function of sex, and so on.

Such comparisons will no doubt be disconcerting to both parties, but they surely ought to be more embarrassing to the secular. For if you are, however mistakenly, committed to the belief that the whole universe is an expression of the intentions of an omnipotent and righteous author, then this belief provides you with a positive reason both for accounting nature good and for speaking of intentions in this connection. But, for anyone who disowns such beliefs, to look to nature as his moral arbiter must be as incongruous and gratuitous as it is for the same person to hope to find some natural law of progress to do substitute duty for Providence (III (iv)–(vi) above). T. H. Huxley in his famous Romanes Lecture on 'Evolution and Ethics' may well have gone too far, particularly in replacing a positive connection by a negative rather than by no connection at all. But for an atheist or an agnostic his sort of approach is, surely, more appropriate: 'Let us understand, once for all, that the ethical progress of society depends, not on imitating the cosmic process, still less in running away from it, but in combating it.'[83]

Waddington has made several essays towards an evolutionary ethics. Indeed he was largely responsible for a revival of interest in the possibilities in Britain during the early 1940s: first by provoking a discussion in *Nature*; and then by editing a consequent book on *Science and Ethics*. We have noticed, and shall notice, his contributions to that book only incidentally: partly because Professor D. D. Raphael has already dealt very faithfully with them as part of his philosopher's contribution to a commemorative volume of *A Century of Darwin*; but mainly because Waddington has since made it clear that he would prefer to be judged by his later work on *The Ethical Animal*. In his contributions to *Science and Ethics* he seemed to be wanting to read norms off immediately from biological descriptions: 'It is a complicated matter to describe what is normal, as opposed to abnormal growth, but it can be done; and, once it is done there is a generally valid criterion of goodness in food. . . .'[84] But in the latter he advocates a rather more sophisticated operation: 'if we investigate by normal scientific methods the way in which the existence of ethical beliefs is involved in the causal nexus of the world's happenings, we shall be forced to conclude that the function of ethicising is to mediate the progress of human evolution. . . . We shall also find that this progress, in the world as a whole, exhibits a direction. . . . Putting these two points together we can define a criterion which does not depend for its validity on any pre-existing ethical belief', and he is most insistent that what is distinctive about his view is that this criterion is 'a criterion for deciding between alternative systems of belief'.[85]

It is hard to determine whether one ought to be more surprised or more distressed that Waddington should think that, by thus making his evolutionary criterion not directly a criterion of the right but rather a criterion for judging which is the best among rival systems of belief about what is right, he escapes objections of the kind we have been deploying. But, once the key passages have been picked out for attention, it is surely obvious that it does not. For what is a criterion for deciding which is best among rival systems of belief about what is right if it is not a means of deciding which set of beliefs is, on balance, the most correct (which exercise obviously necessitates some prior criterion of what is right)? If in reply it is suggested that Waddington's criterion is intended only as a criterion of the efficiency or otherwise of different systems of ethicising [*sic*] in their supposed biological function, 'to mediate the progress of human evolution', then the further question arises, whether the putative direction of human evolution is being taken to be commendable as such, or only in so far as the actual direction satisfies some other standards. If the former, then — in a catch-phrase of the old pre-television era — this is where we came in. If the latter, then, as far as our present sort of evolutionary ethics is concerned, that's that.

V. SEEING IN AN EVOLUTIONARY PERSPECTIVE

It might therefore seem that the conclusions of our long discussion should be what Mrs. Carlyle suggested at the beginning: in her emphatic way she 'did not feel that the slightest light could be thrown on my practical life for me, by having it ever so logically made out that my first ancestor, millions of millions of ages back, had been, or even had not been, an oyster'.[86] Yet even if we discount — as is nowadays generally and perhaps too easily done — any sort of possible implication for questions of religion, Mrs. Carlyle's conclusion is far too abrupt. For we have still to consider a third way of trying to bring the facts of evolutionary biology into relation with practical conclusions for morals and politics.

This third way consists in the relatively modest but nevertheless substantial contention that such practical and present questions can and should be seen in an evolutionary perspective. Julian Huxley, for instance, has in his time — as we have seen (III (iv) and (vi), and IV (ii), above) — explored other and stronger versions of evolutionary ethics. But it is this third contention which has survived and which is the guiding and unifying idea of both *Evolution in Action* (1953) and *Essays of a Humanist* (1964). The Preface to the former urges: 'It makes a great difference whether we think of the history of mankind as wholly apart from the rest of life, or as a continuation of the general evolutionary process, though with special characteristics of its own.'[87] Again, in the latter he writes: 'It is in large measure due to Darwin's work on biological evolution that we now possess this new vision of human destiny . . .'; which destiny 'is to be the chief agent for the future of evolution on this planet'; for, in the striking phrase already quoted from the earlier book, man 'finds himself in the unexpected position of business manager for the cosmic process of evolution'.[88]

But now, if the challenge of Mrs. Carlyle is to be met, two related questions have to be answered, and answered satisfactorily: first, why should the rest of us, who are not by training and inclination biologists, strive to think of things in this way; and second, what 'great difference' is it supposed to make if we do? Certainly, it is entirely natural for a professional biologist to see everything in this sort of perspective; and no doubt it is good for all of us to try from time to time to see things from such other points of view. But is there any reason for thinking that this evolutionary perspective is any more, or any less, valid than whatever might come naturally to someone else schooled in a different discipline? To an astronomer, perhaps, it might be equally natural to see things on scales by which man and life would not appear at all. And to the sort of eloquence about man's cosmic insignificance provoked by such considerations we may recall the robust response of Frank Ramsey, in the spirit of Mrs. Carlyle: 'My picture of the world is drawn in perspective, and not like a model to scale. The foreground is occupied by human beings and the stars are all as small as threepenny bits.'[89]

The first things which need to be said in reply to the challenge is that this evolutionary sort of way of looking at things presupposes various general propositions, and that these are in fact true. There may be some ways of looking at some things, or at all things, with regard to which no issues of truth or falsehood arise at all. But where, as here, they do arise, we surely must insist, as a necessary though not necessarily a sufficient condition of the acceptability of the way in question, that the propositions concerned are either known or reasonably believed to be true (or, of course, justifiably entertained for some legitimate speculative or imaginative purpose). We must not with a too easy catholicity allow, without ever first examining the truth of all their would-be factual presuppositions, that the professional points of view of the astrologer, the psychoanalyst, the theologian, and the evolutionary biologist are all equally valid and acceptable.

For us the relevant general propositions are the claim that the history of mankind is a continuation of the general evolutionary process, and the claim that the future of this entire process — the future of all other living things as well as of mankind — lies largely or wholly in human hands. We have already said something about the second of these two claims (III (vi) above). The first requires a little exposition. For it involves a certain extension and development of the ideas of the *Origin*, the sort of extension and development which Darwin himself began in *The Descent of Man*. The crux is the generalisation of the insistence on the continuity of evolution, the denial of any sort of special creation at any stage, and the application of this to man: 'He who is not content to look, like a savage, at the phenomena of nature as disconnected, cannot any longer believe that man is the work of a special act of creation.'[90]

The full significance of this first claim can, as so often, be best brought out by considering what is being rejected. Darwin wrote, in the final paragraph of his concluding chapter: 'Man may be excused for feeling some pride at having risen, though not through his own exertions, to the very summit of the organic scale. . . . We must, however, acknowledge . . . that man with all his noble qualities . . . with his god-like intellect which has penetrated into the movements and constitution of the solar system. . . . Man still bears in his bodily frame the indelible stamp of his lowly origin.'[91] That qualification 'in his bodily frame' produces an understatement. For the whole argument of the book is against any such limitation which would leave room for the idea of the special creation of incorporeal souls as potentially immortal subjects of the distinctively human attributes. Darwin as much as Huxley was therefore committed to rejecting what is surely an essential doctrine of the Roman Catholic faith: for while — generously — 'the teaching of the Church leaves the doctrine of evolution an open question, as long as it confines its speculations to the development, from other living matter already in existence, of the human body'; nevertheless, 'That souls are immediately created by God is a view which the Catholic faith imposes on us.'[92]

It is nowadays unfashionable to draw attention to such conflicts. Yet they do have to be recognised if we are going to understand how much may be involved in seeing in an evolutionary perspective. This particular conflict is one of the grounds to which we must look to appreciate the soundness of Royce's assessment, quoted on page viii, of the 'importance to philosophy' of Darwin's work: 'Once man himself was accepted as a natural product of the evolutionary process, the rest of the Cartesian compromise could hardly be maintained. It was this obvious extension of the Darwinian theory, rather than the actual argument of the *Origin*, which was the occasion for Bishop Wilberforce's scurrilous attack at the British Association meeting of 1860.'[93] And that Wittgenstein should have even seemed to be denying the importance of these 'philosophical implications of Darwinism' is an indication of an obsessively narrow conception of philosophy: 'The history of ideas is', as one of its masters has remarked, 'no subject for highly departmentalised minds; and it is pursued with some difficulty in an age of departmentalised minds.'[94]

Darwin is thus himself developing in the *Descent* a thesis implicit already in the *Origin*: that man is wholly a part of nature; and that there is no need or warrant to appeal to special interventions to account for any stage or aspect of his origin and development. As applied to ethics in particular this involves that all moral ideas and ideals have originated in the world; and that, having thus in the past been subject to change, they will presumably in the future too, for better or for worse, continue to evolve.

Something must now be said, both about the sense of 'imply' in which the general thesis, as applied to man, is implicit in the *Origin*, and about what is and is not necessarily involved in such a claim that moral ideas and ideals have evolved and will presumably continue to evolve.

First, it is a weak but widespread sense of 'imply', one of special importance in the history of ideas, yet one which because it has had so little attention from philosophers is hard to characterise satisfactorily. We shall try briefly to suggest the sort of thing which is and is not involved, though this weak kind of implication does need far more thorough examination than it can have here. To assert any proposition commits you, on pain of self-contradiction, to accept all the logical consequences of that proposition: for the simple but sufficient reason that 'logical consequence' is defined as something which cannot be denied without contradicting the original assertion. Now the theory of the *Origin* certainly could without difficulty be formulated, even if it is not already, in such a way that an adherent of that theory was not logically required, not required on pain of self-contradiction, to accept the application of its key ideas to our own species — on the lines indicated in the *Descent*. There need, that is to say, be no formal logical inconsistency in at one and the same time asserting the origin of all other species of animals ('the brutes') and of plants by natural selection, while nevertheless denying such an origin for men — or perhaps only for their supposed incorporeal souls.

Nevertheless, even though the application of the original theory (or of the original theory suitably amended) to our species may not in the stronger sense be logically implied, it certainly is in a weaker sense implicit. For, unless some very potent positive reason can be produced for granting a special exemption, the refusal to include mankind in the scope of the theory must be in the last degree arbitrary, and thus unreasonable right up towards the point of, even though it may not actually involve, self-contradiction. Similarly, though it is again surely not actually contradictory to maintain that evolution by natural selection is the means chosen by Omnipotence in order to produce our own privileged species, the contention is at least at first sight — what shall we say? — incongruous. To that extent, and in that sense, a radical and comprehensive naturalism must appear to be implicit in Darwinism. (A few paragraphs back we said that one reason for denying that Darwin's theory had any philosophical implications was a concentration on a very narrow sense of 'philosophy'. We can now add, and a very strict sense of 'implication'.)

Both the positions mentioned in the previous paragraph may instructively be compared with that developed in Philip Gosse's too easily ridiculed and too rarely read book, *The Natural History of Creation* (*Omphalos*). Gosse was writing at a time when uniformitarian and evolutionary views had long since become the almost universally accepted orthodoxy in geology, but when — incongruously, but strictly not inconsistently — most biologists still believed that each species had been independently created. *Omphalos* was in fact published just two years before *The Origin of Species*, in 1857. What Gosse emphasised, and what most of his scientific colleagues chose to forget, was that any special creation of any creature which is to be truly a member of whatever particular species is in question must be a creation at some particular stages in various cycles. Gosse also urged that the same sort of thing applies to geological and other phenomena too. But in so far as this is true, any specially created thing must at the moment of creation contain 'traces' of a past which it has not in fact had. Just as the trunks of specially created trees must, if they are to be true adult specimens of their kinds, have growth rings indicating their annual progress through the years they never had, so also specially created rocks, if they too are to be true specimens of their kinds, must contain their own appropriate 'traces' of their past which never was — including in particular, in some cases, fossils.

To the whole-hearted scientific naturalist such consequences of doctrines of special creation are bound to be altogether incredible; and no doubt Gosse should have seen that he had produced a triumphant reduction to absurdity of an idea incongruous with the whole spirit and method of science. Yet no one who was prepared — as almost all Gosse's contemporaries at the time of the publication of *Omphalos* were — to go on accepting the conventional wisdom about the special creation of species had any business to despise him — as they mostly did — when with learning and candour he presented these consequences as they applied to things organic and inorganic both, and when he honestly and boldly accepted and proclaimed them for true as being indeed clear consequences of other and more fundamental things which he also held for true. *Omphalos* is, of course, the book of a deluded fanatic. But it is neither mean, nor evasive, nor time-serving, nor muddle-headed.

Returning to the *Descent*, our second question is about the bearing of the Darwinian claim that moral ideas and ideals have evolved and presumably will continue to evolve. One thing which is certainly not a necessary consequence of this claim, though it is too often thought that it is, is that all or any moral claims are unimportant and lacking in any sort of authority. Thus to Hume — the first considerable philosopher in the modern period to develop a world-outlook which was through and through secular, this-

E

worldly, and man-centred — to argue that morality is rooted in human needs and human inclinations, and these needs and inclinations which we in some measure share with the higher animals, was the very reverse of depreciatory. This point was taken by Darwin too. It was seen as a sign of grace in him by some of the Victorian first reviewers of the *Descent*.[95] What and all that may be implicit, in the weak if not the strong sense, in the discovery that moral ideas and ideals have evolved, is that moral claims cannot possess any supernatural authority. But that is a very different thing from being unimportant, or lacking any sort of authority at all.

Again, it is not, though it is too often mistaken to be, a part or a consequence of the argument of the *Descent* that human phenomena must be equated with their sub-human origins. It is, therefore, quite wrong to complain: 'Thus, as he earlier reduced language to the grunts and growls of a dog, he now contrived to reduce religion to the lick of the dog's tongue and the wagging of his tail.'[96] Not merely is such an equation not a part or consequence of, it must be strictly incompatible with, an evolutionary doctrine. For evolution entails change and, unless the process of change has turned full circle, this entails difference — which means that, with that one biologically irrelevant exception, if A has evolved from B, A cannot be the same as B.

On the other hand what is, surely, at least in the weak sense, implicit in a vision of ethics as subject to evolution is, first, a critical approach to all first-order moral issues and second, an insistence on completely naturalistic answers to second-order questions about the nature of ethics. No doubt one could, without any strict and formal inconsistency, allow moral evolution, for better and for worse, to be a fact, while still insisting that some favoured actual moral norms are not merely right — which some indeed surely are — but somehow in principle beyond all need for justification and all possibility of criticism. The epistemological correlate of such a view will usually be that the favoured norms are recognised as the right ones by (favoured) intuition. No doubt too it could similarly be strictly consistent to admit the same general fact while still maintaining that some particular known standards are in some way divinely revealed and endorsed. Yet either or both these positions must surely be awkward and uncomfortable — wide open to charges of arbitrariness and special pleading.

By contrast, other approaches to moral questions and accounts of their nature — those of Hume, for instance — can accommodate themselves very comfortably with the fact of general and moral evolution; and indeed some — Hume again provides an example — might almost seem to demand an evolutionary background. An example of the other sort would be *Principia Ethica*. For Moore's book, though he presumably had the advantage of knowing and accepting the main lines of Darwin's thought, is, as has frequently been observed, curiously parochial. The argument proceeds as it were in suspense outside space and time; and, incidentally, in complete isolation from the progress of the natural and the human sciences. The values which were to prove so acceptable to Bloomsbury seem to be taken as luminously self-evident.[97] Such 'Intuitionist ethics is a kind of secularised version of the ethics of Divine command in which the supernatural lawgiver is internalised . . .';[98] and in this it, like its unsecularised original, is incongruous, though not necessarily incompatible, with the facts of human evolution.

This then provides the first and most extensive part of the answer to Mrs. Carlyle. The case for urging the need to see morality — or anything else — in an evolutionary perspective must, of course, start from the contention that an evolutionary account of its genesis and future is in fact correct; and in this philosophical context we have throughout been taking the truth of that surely not very seriously disputatious scientific contention for granted. But if once we do grant this, and — to adapt a phrase used by Mrs. Carlyle's husband — 'Gad! we'd better!', then it has certain implications both for ethics and for meta-ethics, in the weak but important sense of 'implication' rather sketchily explained above.

Two other lines of justification can be dealt with here very shortly, though the relative brevity is not necessarily an indication of relative unimportance. Both are the sorts of justification which can be, and tediously but none the less truly often are, offered for 'taking the wider view'. The first is that it may enable us to see things which do not emerge so easily, or perhaps at all, if we limit ourselves to a more parochial survey. Julian Huxley again constitutes an excellent example. For it was precisely his evolutionary vision which enabled him to recognise clearly, long locust years before this was even as widely admitted as it now is, that human fertility represents the number-one threat to the present and future welfare of the human race. It is this same evolutionary vision, rooted in the facts of biology, which links this human concern with a driving anxiety for the conservation of wild life, and which also opens up an awareness of the possibilities of eugenics as a challenge to research and action.[99]

The second is that some men have a longing 'to see things as a whole', to find some deep, comprehensive, unifying perspective against which they may set their everyday lives. No philosopher can afford either to despise or not to share such yearnings; and the evolutionary vision possesses the certainly neither universal nor despicable merit of being based upon, and not incompatible with any, known facts. The passage of Julian Huxley from which we have quoted already will bear repetition in full: 'In the light of evolutionary biology man can now see himself as the sole agent of further evolutionary advance on this planet, and one of the few possible instruments of progress in the universe at large. He finds himself in the unexpected position of business manager for the cosmic process of evolution. He no longer ought to feel separated from the rest of nature, for he is part of it — that part which has become conscious, capable of love and understanding and aspiration. He need no longer regard himself as insignificant in relation to the cosmos.'[100]

NOTES

The references in these notes are for the sake of brevity all given by the name of the author only, followed where necessary by an arabic number in brackets to indicate which work is referred to, and then the page number or the number of the chapter and/or section in point. The Bibliography provides the key needed for the interpretation of these references.

I should also like here to thank Dr. W. D. Hudson, the General Editor of the present series, Professor R. F. Atkinson, at that time still a colleague at Keele, Mr. John Grundy, and Miss Faith Heathcote for reading this whole study in draft and for making a large number of suggestions. These have in sum led to a substantial improvement in the final version as now published.

1. Spencer, vol. i, p. viii; punctuation adjusted.
2. Ritchie, § 1.
3. Malthus, p. 17.
4. Wittgenstein, p. 29.
5. Toulmin, p. 465.
6. Engels, pp. 19, 208–10; but cf. Willey, pp. 14 ff.
7. Quoted in Hofstadter, p. 31. It is wholly appropriate that this quotation should be found in a chapter on 'The Vogue of Spencer'. For Herbert Spencer too was an advocate of self-reliant individualism in a freely competitive economy, always boasted of being an evolutionary thinker, and had an enormous influence in the U.S.A. Hofstadter's source is W. J. Ghent, *Our Benevolent Feudalism* (Macmillan, New York, 1902), and Ghent's, as I know, thanks to my colleague Mr. Francis Celoria, who examined the British Museum copy for me, is anonymous: 'Mr. Rockefeller appeals both to evolution and to divine sanction . . . he is reported as declaring in one of his Sunday-school addresses. . . .' (Ghent, p. 29).
8. Marx (1).
9. Ferri, p. v.
10. Ibid., pp. vii–viii.
11. Ibid., p. 1.
12. Ibid., pp. 136, 140.
13. Lovejoy (2), p. 268; cf. Lovejoy (1), *passim*.
14. Lucretius, v. 790–2, 832–5, 837–41, 845–8, 855–9.
15. Kirk and Raven, pp. 336–40.
16. Darwin (3), p. 140.
17. Pantin, p. 137; italics in original. In the next few paragraphs I retraverse some, but only some, of the ground covered in an earlier essay on 'The Structure of Darwinism' (Flew (2)).
18. Darwin (1), p. 2.
19. Ibid., p. 3.
20. Ibid.; the italics are as in the original, but here and elsewhere the capitalisation and inverted commas in quotations have been made to conform with the conventions followed in the rest of the present study.

21. Darwin (1), p. 50.

22. Ibid., pp. 102–3.

23. E. Gosse, pp. 66 ff.; cf. P. Gosse, *passim*.

24. Darwin (1), p. 4.

25. Ibid., p. 131.

26. Darwin (2), p. viii.

27. Darwin (1), pp. 413–14.

28. Ibid., pp. 424–5.

29. Ritchie, p. 76.

30. Ibid., pp. 12–13, 28.

31. Darwin (1), pp. 102–3.

32. See, for instance, Spencer, vol. ii, *passim*; and cf. Hofstadter, ch. 2.

33. See, for supporting argument, Flew (6), ch. 2.

34. See, for supporting argument, Flew (1).

35. Manser; and cf. Flew (5).

36. Tennyson, p. 243.

37. Hegel, p. 216, and cf. p. 375; the phrase is actually an unacknowledged borrowing from Schiller.

38. Darwin (1), pp. 234, 428.

39. Auden, p. 119.

40. Darwin and Seward, vol. i, p. 114 n.

41. Marx (2), p. xix.

42. J. S. Huxley (1), pp. 17, 19, 58.

43. Ibid., pp. 34, 35, 59.

44. Ibid., pp. 78–79.

45. Spender and Lehmann, p. 56.

46. Needham (1), pp. 16, 41, 266; italics in both cases original.

47. Needham (2), pp. 209–10.

48. Needham (1), pp. 266 ff.

49. Dutt, in *The Communist International* for 1935; quoted in Needham (1), p. 267.

50. For further development of this theme in this and similar contexts see Flew (3), ch. 6.

51. Cornforth, pp. 332–3.

52. Quinton, p. 120.

53. J. S. Huxley (3), p. 132.

54. Needham (1), pp. 32 ff., 160 ff., 243 ff., and *passim*.

55. Spender and Lehmann, pp. 56, 58.

56. Darwin (1), p. 429.

57. Chandler, p. 46.

58. Himmelfarb, p. 351.

59. See Manser; and cf. Flew (5).

60. Trevor-Roper, pp. 39, 51; and cf., perhaps more accessibly, Bullock, pp. 36, 89, 398–9, 672, 693.

61. Booth, p. 44; T. H. Huxley, perhaps a trifle unfairly, drew attention to this passage in a letter to *The Times* on 29 December 1890.

62. Peirce, vol. vi, pp. 293, 298.

63. See MacIntyre, Atkinson, Hunter, and Flew and Hunter; the whole controversy is now conveniently collected in Chappell, pp. 240–307.

64. See Searle; and cf. Flew (4).

65. Quinton, pp. 110–11; punctuation made to conform.

66. Einstein, p. 114.

67. J. S. Huxley (2), p. 124.

68. Ibid., pp. 125, 214.

69. Spender, vol. ii, pp. vi, 25, 260.

70. Ibid., vol. i, pp. 25 (italics supplied), 46; vol. ii, p. 432.

71. T. H. Huxley (2), p. 80.

72. Russell, p. 24.

73. Quillian, pp. 78, 95.

74. See especially ibid., p. 137; and cf. p. 109.

75. Moore, pp. 38, 39–40.

76. Ibid., p. 41; italics in original.

77. Hume (1), title-page.

78. Newton, especially pp. 124–5; the same, idea is, of course, found earlier — in Galileo, for instance, and among the Greek atomists.

79. Hume (2), p. 23 n.

80. Needham (1), pp. 151 (italics supplied), 56.

81. Ibid., p. 56.

82. Waddington (1), p. 125. Entirely by the way: if we are going to bring in pre-Columbian Mexico — or anything else — let us get it right. The author on the previous page conjures up 'an Aztec of Chicken [*sic*] Itza', whereas in fact Chichen Itza was founded by the Maya, was later taken over by the Toltecs, but was never Aztec.

83. T. H. Huxley (2), p. 82.

84. Waddington (1), p. 41.

85. Waddington (2), pp. 59, 173.

86. Carlyle, vol. iii pp. 20–21.

87. J. S. Huxley (3), p. vii.

88. J. S. Huxley (4), pp. 37, 132.

89. Ramsey, p. 291; and cf. Flew and Hepburn.

90. Darwin (2), p. 927.

91. Ibid., pp. 946–7.

92. Pius XII, p. 30.

93. Toulmin and Goodfield, p. 240.

94. Lovejoy (2), p. 22.

95. For the references, see the notes to pp. 294–5 of Himmelfarb.
96. Himmelfarb, p. 307.
97. Moore, especially ch. 6; and cf. Keynes.
98. Quinton, p. 128.
99. J. S. Huxley (4), *passim*.
100. J. S. Huxley (3), p. 132.

SELECT BIBLIOGRAPHY

We have tried to notice in the text all the works which in compiling the present study we have found useful, and some others too. This Select Bibliography therefore draws special attention to a few of these works, marked with an asterisk in the General Bibliography, where their full particulars will be found. The basic points of reference should, for reasons given in the text, be two works of Darwin: first, *The Origin of Species*, especially chap. xiv; and second, *The Descent of Man*, part I, especially chapts. iii and iv.

For a survey of the actual impact of Darwinian ideas, or ideas thought to be Darwinian, on moral and political thinking in one country see Hofstadter's *Social Darwinism in American Thought* (*1860–1915*). Two other historical studies can also be recommended: first, Quillian's *The Moral Theory of Evolutionary Naturalism*; and second, Wiener's *Evolution and the Founders of Pragmatism*. A useful secondary source for accounts of the ideas of a baker's dozen of nineteenth-century contributors to *Evolutional Ethics* is part I of the book of that title by C. M. Williams; and its part II constitutes a specimen of the sort of thing usually involved, a specimen none the less valuable for this purpose for being from the pen of a writer very definitely not of the first rank.

Such primary sources as Spencer's *The Principles of Ethics* or Stephen's *The Science of Ethics* generally make protracted and unrewarding reading. But this certainly does not apply to T. H. Huxley's Romanes Lecture on 'Evolution and Ethics', re-issued along with various pieces by his grandson as a book under the same title. T. H. Huxley's acceptance of a gladiatorial view of sub-human nature, and his deliberate rejection of this as a human ideal, can be most interestingly contrasted with Kropotkin's stress on *Mutual Aid* at the sub-human as well as the human level, and the contention in his *Ethics* 'that not only does Nature fail to give us a lesson of amoralism . . . but . . . *the very ideas of bad and good . . .*

have been borrowed from Nature' (p. 16; italics original). In studying Bagehot's curiously titled *Physics and Politics* it is salutary to read the author's remarks on 'unfit men and beaten races' aloud in a German accent. Among works wholly of our century we can for the various reasons indicated in the text recommend Needham's *Time: the Refreshing River*, Julian Huxley's *Essays of a Humanist*, and Waddington's *Science and Ethics*.

GENERAL BIBLIOGRAPHY

Atkinson, R. F., '"Hume on *is* and *ought*": a Reply to Mr. MacIntyre,' *Philosophical Review*, vol. lxx (1961).

Auden, W. H., *Collected Shorter Poems* (1930–1944), (Faber, London, 1950).

Bagehot, W., *Physics and Politics*, ed. J. Barzun (Knopf, New York, 1948).

Booth, W., *In Darkest England, and the Way Out* (Salvation Army, London, 1890).

Bullock, A., *Hitler: a Study in Tyranny* (Penguin Books, Harmondsworth, 1962).

Carlyle, J. W., *Letters and Memorials* (Longmans, Green, London, 1883).

Chambers, R., *Vestiges of the Natural History of Creation* (12th edn., 1844; W. & R. Chambers, London and Edinburgh, 1884).

Chandler, R., *Farewell, My Lovely* (Penguin Books, Harmondsworth, 1949).

Chappell, V. C. (ed.), *Hume, a Collection of Critical Essays* (Doubleday–Anchor, New York, 1966; Macmillan, London, 1968).

Cornforth, M., *Marxism and the Linguistic Philosophy* (Lawrence & Wishart, London, 1965).

*Darwin, C. (1), *The Origin of Species* (6th edn., J. Murray, London, 1872).

—— (2), *The Descent of Man* (new edn., J. Murray, London, 1901).